PowerUp

The Twelve Powers Revisited as
Accelerated Abilities

Paul Hasselbeck
Cher Holton

Prosperity Publishing House

Copyright ©2010 Paul Hasselbeck and Cher Holton

All rights reserved.

Reproduction or translation of any part of this work beyond that permitted by Section 107 or 108 of the 1976 United States Copyright Act without the permission of the copyright owner is unlawful. Requests for permission or further information should be addressed to the authors, c/o Prosperity Publishing House, 1405 Autumn Ridge Drive, Durham. NC 27712.

This publication is designed to provide accurate and authoritative information in regard to the subject matter covered. It is sold with the understanding that the publisher is not engaged in rendering legal, accounting, or other professional service. If legal advice or other expert assistance is required, the services of a competent professional person should be sought. *From a Declaration of Principles jointly adopted by a Committee of the American Bar Association and a Committee of Publishers.*

Prosperity Publishing House
Durham, NC

Library of Congress Cataloging-in-Publication Data

Hasselbeck, Paul
PowerUp : The Twelve Powers revisited as accelerated abilities / Paul Hasselbeck and Cher Holton
    p. cm.
    Includes bibliographical references.
    ISBN 978-1-893095-64-9
    1. Spiritual   2. New Thought   3. Self Help
    II. Title

Library of Congress Control Number: 2010907974
Printed in the United States of America

10 9 8 7 6 5 4 3 2 1
6th printing 2012

Table of Contents

12 Powers Chart v

Introduction 1

How the Twelve Abilities Operate 4

How to Read This Book 5

Putting It Into Practice 7

Faith 9

   Faith: Putting It Into Practice 18

Strength 23

   Strength: Putting It Into Practice 30

Judgment/Wisdom 33

   Judgment/Wisdom: Putting It Into Practice 42

Love 45

   Love: Putting It Into Practice 53

Power/Dominion 57

   Power/Dominion: Putting It Into Practice 63

Imagination 65

   Imagination: Putting It Into Practice 70

Understanding 73

   Understanding: Putting It Into Practice 78

Will 81

   Will: Putting It Into Practice 88

Order 91

   Order: Putting It Into Practice 96

Zeal/Enthusiasm 99

   Zeal: Putting It Into Practice 106

Elimination/Release 109

   Elimination: Putting It Into Practice 116

Life 119

   Life: Putting It Into Practice 125

Case Example: Mary 127

Appendices

   Appendix 1: Historical Background on the Twelve Powers . . .134

Appendix 2: Unregenerate, Degeneration, Generation,
  and Regeneration *135*
Appendix 3: Additional Commentaries
  Colors Associated with the Powers *146*
  Disciples and the Powers *146*
  Body Locations Associated with the Powers *146*
Appendix 4: Twelve Powers/Abilities Summary Chart *148*
Appendix 5: Twelve Powers with Adverse Meanings Chart . . .*150*

About the Authors *151*
Other Books/Products *152*

The Twelve Powers/Abilities

You have within you twelve incredible Powers, which have their own special Abilities and can be developed and called upon to empower and transform your life!

Faith
Royal Blue – Peter
Pineal Gland
Ability to Believe with Confidence, Have Conviction

Understanding
Gold – Thomas
Front Brain
Ability to Know, Perceive

Will
Silver – Matthew
Front Brain
Ability to Choose, Decide, Lead

Imagination
Light Blue – Bartholomew
Between the Eyes
Ability to Image, Envision, Dream, Conceptualize

Dominion
Purple – Philip
Root of Tongue; Larynx
Ability to Master, Dominate, Control

Wisdom/Judgment
Yellow – James, son of Zebedee
Solar Plexus
Ability to Evaluate, Discern, Appraise, Apply What You Know

Order
Olive Green – James, son of Alphaeus
Back of Navel
Ability to Organize, Balance, Sequence,

Life
Red – Judas
Reproductive Center
Ability to Energize, Vitalize, Enliven, BeWhole and Healthy

Zeal
Orange – Simon the Zealot
Brain Stem
Ability to be Passionate, to Start, to Motivate

Love
Pink – John
Back of Heart
Ability to Harmonize, Unify, and Attract

Strength
Spring Green – Andrew
Small of Back
Ability to Endure, Stay the Course, Persist, Persevere

Elimination
Russet – Thaddeus
Lower Intestinal Region
Ability to Release, Deny, Let Go

© 2010 Prosperity Publishing House

Introduction

Within each person there is a new world waiting discovery, a world in which there are capabilities of unlimited strength, perfect knowing, radiant life, and other latent abilities beyond our greatest present capacity to conceive.

~ Winifred Wilkinson Hausmann
Your God-Given Potential, p. 24

*ℐ*magine being able to live life more fully, more consciously, more masterfully. Imagine expressing your true Christ nature in every situation you experience. Imagine being the best person or best Christ you can be! This book is designed to give you powerful tools for doing just that — thus transforming your life.

The foundational ideas presented in this book are derived from the work of Charles Fillmore in his book, *The Twelve Powers of Man*, first published in 1930. Since then, much has been said and written about the Twelve Powers. What seemed to be missing was an easy-to-understand guide for the practical application and use of these Twelve Powers in everyday life.

This book is not meant to be a comprehensive study of the Twelve Powers, although supporting information and resources are provided in the appendices for those who want to dive deeper. Just a word of caution: as you read about the Twelve Powers from various sources, you will find contradictions and/or paradoxes. Sometimes this even happens within the same text! For example: Charles Fillmore defines Faith as the "perceiving power of the mind linked with the power to shape substance." One could argue that the perceiving power of the mind is Understanding, while the ability to shape substance is Imagination. Thus, it may seem that Faith is defined as the combined Abilities of Understanding and Imagination. In cases like this, as you read books on the Twelve Powers, we invite you to take a deep breath and reflect on how these contradictions and paradoxes might be pointing toward a higher understanding that both transcends and includes them.

In our experience, the Twelve Powers are sometimes confused with other related and tangential concepts that only serve to cloud their practical use. One example is the Power of Will, which is essentially the ability to choose. It is frequently equated with the traditional view of a God that has a specific will for each and every person (God's Will) — a choice that has already been made. As you can see, they are related but not exactly the same.

It is our assertion that a person is always using the Twelve Powers, either consciously or subconsciously. Our intention with this book is to simplify and clarify each of the Powers, creating easily understood and practical ways to apply them in our everyday lives. In doing this, we prefer to call them Twelve Abilities rather than the traditional term "Powers," which dates to the early part of the last century. We believe "Abilities" is better understood in today's language, and exemplifies the practical application, which is the focus of this book.

For the purposes of this book, we will be looking at each Ability individually, even though they work together as One. This is much like a student automobile mechanic who studies each part of an engine to understand how the individual components work in conjunction with each other. For example, a battery holds an electrical charge that provides the electricity for a spark plug which produces the spark igniting the fuel in the cylinder. These are just three components of an engine that work together to produce the power to propel an automobile down the highway. In a similar way, each of our Twelve Powers/Abilities has a role to play, and together they work in concert to support one another as we master the art of living.

How the Twelve Abilities Operate

It is important to realize that our Twelve Powers, or Abilities, do not care how they are used. They are simply Spiritual Ideas, and are available regardless of who the person is or what the intent might be. A good analogy from our physical world is the idea of table. The idea of table does not care how it is used. It does not care how much money a person makes, what job the person has, or even what belief system the person practices. It simply is. Each person who uses the idea of table decides what kind a table is built. in terms of shape, size, color, function, etc.

In a similar way, we can use these Spiritual Abilities to experience the good, the bad, or the ugly. The choice is always ours. It is much like humor. We could think of humor as the capability to be funny; each of us determines how we use humor according to our own level of consciousness. Humor does not come with one preset and predetermined way in which it must be used. It simply is. The use of humor is up to the person making the joke and then it is interpreted by the listener. It can be used to uplift, or it can be used to put people down and demean them. We can use it in the highest, most uplifting ways, or we could choose to use it in "mean spirited" ways. The choice is always ours!

How to Read This Book

Each chapter of this book is structured to help you, the reader, understand a particular Power/Ability from several points of view. In addition to describing the Ability, and sharing examples of how it can be used, we will also explore the impact of an Ability that is either underdeveloped or overdeveloped. An Underdeveloped Ability indicates a person who fails to call on the Power/Ability that would allow him/her to effectively handle the situation, and as a result, experiences consequences that are less than desirable. For example, a person with an underdeveloped Ability of Order might have a very messy home or office. While feeling frustrated about the disorder, he/she does not do anything to correct the situation.

On the other hand, when a Power/Ability is overdeveloped, but not coming from the highest, most elevated consciousness, it can come across in a way that is ineffective and overbearing, which also creates consequences that are less than desirable. For example, a person with an overactive Ability of Order might be obsessive compulsive about orderliness in their home or office, and become ridiculously critical if one paper is moved out of place.

Obviously, the goal is to learn how to use each Power/Ability from the most elevated level of consciousness, for the highest and best outcomes in your life.

Here's what's really interesting. All these Abilities, or Powers, are at work within us, all the time! This means they can be used entirely unconsciously. In fact, this is how most people use these Abilities until they become aware of them. Unconsciously, we can use these Abilities either productively or unproductively. For instance, Will, our ability to choose, can be used to make wise and productive choices, or used to make really bad decisions. What's also interesting is that a person may be using some of the Abilities unconsciously, and at the same time using others consciously.

When used consciously, the Powers, or Abilities, can be used from several levels. As you read through these levels, notice that within each level you always have the option of choosing to use the Ability in a positive, more effective way, or in a debilitating, less effective way. As we've said a few times already (and you'll hear it often throughout this book), the choice is always yours! Here are four levels we will explore for each Ability, as we move through this book:

- **We can use the Powers/Abilities from an unconscious level**, based on a cause in subconscious mind which consists of beliefs that are not in our moment-to-moment awareness. This includes choices we make without thinking, when we are operating from an emotional "default" position. If someone asked us why we did something, we probably could not even explain our reasoning. Our embedded theology (the theology of our childhood and other theological systems we have studied) can create many subconscious beliefs, as can traditions and experiences from our families of origin.

- **We can use the Powers/Abilities consciously from our senses,** based on something in physicality we are gleaning through our sight, sound, scent, touch, and/or taste. We may take a free dance class, and because of that experience, decide to pursue dance as an avocation (or decide to never don dance shoes again)! The taste of a certain food may cause us to develop an addiction to it; hearing a certain news broadcast may stimulate us to text in a donation for a worthy cause.

- **We can choose to use the Powers/Abilities consciously from our human personality,** based on thoughts, feelings, attitudes, and/or beliefs held in human consciousness. Our use of denials and affirmations is a good illustration of this level. Another example, from a less empowering consciousness, would be a belief in a fear we hold.

- **From the highest level of consciousness we can muster, we can choose to use these Abilities consciously from our True Identity, or Higher Self,** based upon Divine Ideas, Laws, and Principles. We employ the Abilities in order to more fully express our innate Divine Nature, to be the best person or the best Christ we can be.

Putting It Into Practice

The final section of each chapter is devoted to practical ways to apply the Powers/Abilities in everyday life. As you progress through this 12-week study of the Twelve Powers/Abilities, we want you to integrate the abilities into your life in a deliberate, conscious way. To do this, we invite you to **choose one specific area in your current experience that you want to create, enhance, or change.** It could be a habit, a skill, a financial issue, a goal to achieve, etc. You get the idea! The key is you will be focusing on this specific item throughout this 12-week process, tracking your improvement as you learn how to appropriately apply each new Power/Ability. So be sure to choose something really important to you and that you have primary control over! Here are a few specific examples, to give you an idea of what you might select:

- Achieve an ideal body weight/image
- Create a flow of prosperity (or even more specifically, pay your bills and have enough money for fun things!)
- Eliminate a habit such as smoking, nail biting, or dependence on pain medication
- Learn a new skill, such as dancing or playing the piano
- Travel more
- Obtain the right job
- Go for the Gold! Be the best Christ you can be!

The list of possibilities is endless! So invest some time right now, and decide what you would like to work on during your 12-week study. Remember everything begins and ends with mind or consciousness. Do you want to stop something in your life? Use your mind/consciousness. Do you want to start something in your life? Use your mind/consciousness. Once you have decided, capture it in the box below:

> The specific area I want to focus on throughout my 12-week study of the Twelve Powers/Abilities is:
>
> _____
>
> _____
>
> _____
>
> *I am ready to "PowerUp" my abilities and*
> *master the art of living!*

It is the application of the Powers/Abilities in your everyday life that deepens your understanding of them. The more you consciously use them, the more practical they become! As you progress through this book, we know that you will transform your life.

Faith

Ability to believe, spiritually intuit, perceive, to "hear," and to have conviction

Color: Royal Blue

Apostle: Peter

Location: Pineal Gland (center of brain)

I claim Faith now. I believe I am the best Christ I can be.

Faith is that quality in us which enables us to look past appearances of lack, limitation, or difficulty, to take hold of the divine idea and believe in it even though we do not see any evidence of it except in our mind. Through Faith, we know with an inner knowing the Truth that has not yet expressed in our manifest world.

~ Winnifred Wilkinson Hausmann,
Your God Given Potential, p.38

Faith

Overview

- Apostle: Peter
- Location: At the pineal gland, center of the brain. The pineal gland is sometimes called the master gland. Faith is located here because faith is our ability to believe, and our beliefs determine how we think, feel, and act in any given situation.
- Color: Royal Blue

FAITH is the ability to believe, spiritually intuit, perceive, to "hear," and to have conviction.

From ego/personality: The ability to believe, spiritually intuit, perceive, to "hear," and to have conviction based on our senses, thoughts, feelings, and beliefs. We use FAITH to believe in the law of the land or to believe our fears are real. (When we were kids, we might have believed in a boogeyman under the bed!)

- *Underdeveloped Faith* results in distrust, doubt, misgiving, skepticism, suspicion, and simply an overall inability to believe anything.

- *Overdeveloped Faith* results in being narrow minded, dogmatic, or doctrinaire.

From elevated consciousness: The ability to believe, spiritually intuit, perceive, to "hear," and to have conviction based on Ideas, Truths, Principles, and Laws that are Divine in nature. We use FAITH to be the best person and/or Christ we can be, regardless of outer appearances.

If we planted an apple seed, can you believe we would actually get an apple tree? If we squeezed an orange, can you believe we'd actually get orange juice?

If we visualize an abundant flow of prosperity flowing from our innate awareness of an aspect of Oneness being Divine Substance, can you believe we would actually see a manifestation of prosperity? Ah, that one is a little tougher, isn't it?

Why is it so easy to believe, without doubt, that apple seeds produce apple trees, and oranges produce orange juice — but so difficult to believe we can claim Divine Substance to manifest everything we ever need in terms of our supply? Maybe it has something to do with what we have actually seen and experienced, versus what we have been told, but haven't actually experienced.

This truly is the foundation of Faith! In John 20:29, Jesus said to Thomas, "...because you have seen me, you have believed; blessed are they who have not seen, and yet have believed."

Believing even when we have not seen: that's faith. But it is really important to recognize that Faith is a powerful essence which we can develop and grow. We get critical of ourselves when it appears we don't have the faith we think we should, and beat ourselves up. But look at how you handle other growth areas in your life.

If you decide to learn to play the piano, do you sit down and expect to play Mozart perfectly on your first sitting? If you decide to take up golf or tennis, do you expect to walk in and hit the perfect drive or land the perfect serve on your first lesson? If you decide to take up ballroom dancing, do you expect to go out on the dance floor and do a professional-level routine your first day out? Of course not! Whenever we take up a new skill or hobby, we realize there is a learning curve, and we go in expecting — and allowing — ourselves to be bad before we get good! We know we will go through a period of seeing our ability grow, as we willingly put in the time to practice and learn. And we also discover that with each thing we learn, there is another level to tackle. There's always more to learn. Even professionals work with coaches, as they continue to refine and perfect their skills, always pushing the envelop and discovering new and better ways to do things in their chosen field.

Why should the development of our Faith faculty be any different? So here's what you need to know about faith. First of all: *You never have no faith!* In other words, you *always* have Faith! Faith is one of the Divine Abilities inherent within us. It is *our* responsibility to quicken or strengthen it. So we are really being incorrect when we say, "I lost my faith or I don't have any faith." You cannot lose your faith — you might just have forgotten how to call upon it. The comforting knowledge is that your faith is always there, just waiting to be developed.

Emilie Cady, in her masterpiece *Lessons In Truth*, talks about the different levels of faith. From her work, we have created a kind of continuum of faith, which helps us identify where we are in a certain situation— and also helps us recognize the Truth of where we can be. Here's how it works:

We begin with **Hope**. Hope takes a lot of flack in spiritual circles as a kind of cop out, but we want to go on record saying hope is an important element on our spiritual journey, because hope provides the stimulus to keep people moving forward when otherwise they may give up. It's kind of like our training wheels! And when we don't have a really strongly developed Faith Ability, hope is the light at the end of the tunnel that keeps our journey going in the right direction! You hear people say things like, "Don't give them false hope." We personally believe there is no such thing as false hope. There are lies and wishful thinking, but if there is hope, it is real and powerful and affirming.

So why don't we just want to operate at the hope level? When we work from a basis of hope, we tend to live in a fearful state, concerned that we may or may not receive. And in the Hope state, we fall into the habit of seeing our affirmations, dream boards, and visualizations as magic bullets. If we don't say it just right, or create it perfectly, we won't manifest the result. But it's a start, and we've all been there (and at different times in different situations, we may even revisit!)

We want to move up the Faith Ladder, moving into **Blind Faith**. Blind Faith is where we move forward, instinctively feeling that wherever we are, God is, and all is well. There is light at the end of the tunnel, and we don't know how or why, but we just believe things will work out. This Blind Faith is higher than hope on our continuum, because it is based on Truth, but we may find a need to reassure ourselves often that it will work; it may be hit and miss, and we may question it often when we don't see the results we expect as quickly as we expect them. But the important thing is that we persist, and continue to hold strong to the Truth we believe and use the tools, even if we aren't sure why. Blind Faith feels kind of like magic – but it is only magic until we know how it is done!

As we grow and learn, we are able to move to the highest level of Faith—**Understanding Faith**. This is where we know and understand that there are Spiritual Laws as immutable as physical laws seem to be. They both may sometimes appear unpredictable – but only because they are not totally understood.

Once we realize that Spiritual Laws operate the same way, we move into that powerful level of Understanding Faith, where we can be just as certain that when we apply Spiritual Laws, we are assured of the results that will follow. And that brings us to one other similarity between our apple seed and our orange analogies: you have to do something to get the desired result. To quote Emilie Cady, as she shared in *Lessons In Truth:*

> One of the unerring truths in the universe ... is that the supply of every good always awaits the demand. Another truth is that the demand must be made before the supply can come forth. [You could have a bank account filled with money, but the only way to access it is to request a withdrawal.] To recognize these two statements of Truth and to affirm them are the whole secret of Understanding faith—Faith based on principle! [p. 77]

When we operate from Understanding Faith, we can say, "We have the funds and resources necessary to move forward with this project" with as much conviction as we say, "We squeeze this orange and get orange juice!"

Faith is an innate ability, the vehicle through which each of us believes, intuits, and perceives. Conviction is based on what we believe.

Let's begin by taking a practical look at Faith in our everyday lives. There is Faith based on an appropriate interpretation of our senses, thoughts, and feelings:

- We have Faith based on true information we have been told, learned, and experienced, like having Faith that a particular set of ingredients, measured, combined, and prepared in a certain way, will produce an incredibly delicious cake that's been a family recipe for generations!

- We have Faith we can accomplish certain tasks based on our experience. For example, most of us have ridden a bike or driven a car before, and have Faith we can do it again.

- We have Faith we can learn new things based upon our past experience of successfully mastering something new.

We also have Faith that is based on an *erroneous* interpretation or understanding of our senses, thoughts, and feelings:

- There was a person who saw rats squeezing through some very small holes in a fence. Based on his interpretation of that experience, he believed rats had no bones. Faith in this belief was so strong, no discussion of the fact that a rat is a mammal with an internal skeleton would deter him from this belief.

- Children and adults see scary movies and then, when there is a strange sound in the house, they believe something awful is going to happen.

- Children believe in boogeymen under the bed or in the closet. No matter how much an adult tries to change this belief, a child holds on to it as a means of protection. Consider this illustration: A young boy lived where there was a detached garage far from the house. Every evening he would put his bike away in the dark garage. Every evening he was fearful when he put the bike away because he believed, had Faith, that there was someone in the garage who was going to grab him. The boy held on to this belief, and as an adult is still afraid of the dark, even after years and years of putting that bike away with nothing happening. In spite of all the evidence indicating there was nothing to fear, he still held on to the belief.

- Faith can also show up as prejudices and stereotypes based on the interpretation of information gathered from our senses, thoughts, and feelings. A person can have Faith in one particular car manufacturer or political party, simply based on what was learned from the family of origin.

In each of these cases, there is conviction based on where a person places his or her Faith.

Faith can also be cultivated from a higher state of consciousness. Again, there can be the simple Blind Faith in God, or Higher Power, that is somehow working everything out for good despite our clumsy human actions and interventions. Or, there can be an Understanding Faith, based on the knowledge and experience of Ideas, Truths, Principles, and Laws that are Divine in nature.

- In **Blind Faith**, a person simply trusts that everything is working out for good. In this Blind Faith there is a kind of abdication of responsibility because the belief is that God will somehow intervene.

  For example, if a person really wants something, and in the moment decides not to buy it, s/he might say something like, "It will be mine if it is meant to be." This expresses the belief of having Faith in a God or Universe that decides whether s/he gets it.

- In **Understanding Faith**, a person takes more personal responsibility for the understanding and application of Divine Ideas, Truths, Principles, and Laws that are Divine in Nature. This person sees what is wanted and consciously uses the Divine Laws and Principles in order to have it.

An underdeveloped Faith results in a person who exhibits distrust, doubt, misgiving, skepticism, or suspicion. It may also manifest as a person with an overall inability to believe anything. S/he is always questioning everything anyone else says, and often lives in fear, regardless of how much data to the contrary is presented.

An overdeveloped Faith, on the other hand, results in a person being narrow minded, dogmatic, or doctrinaire. We're sure you've encountered people who walk around with the attitude that says, "My mind is made up! Don't confuse me with the facts!"

Let's look at Faith in another way. Faith (along with all the other Abilities) can be expressed from four different levels of consciousness:

1. **Unconscious Faith:** based on a cause in subconscious mind which consists of beliefs that are not in our moment to moment aware-ness. A person may know the beliefs exist, and simply forget about them during daily activities. For instance, when driving, many women have a habit of stretching out their right arm across the seat when there is a need to stop quickly. It comes from the unconscious belief that the driver had to protect the child from crashing into the windshield (a 'throwback belief' to a time before we had seatbelts and laws about children riding in the front seat).

2. **Conscious Faith from our senses:** based on something in physi-cality we are gleaning through our sight, sound, scent, touch, and/or taste. An example would be a man who takes a class in scuba div-ing, and experiences the way the safety equipment works. He then trusts the equipment and is able to scuba dive confidently.

3. **Conscious Faith from our human personality:** based on thoughts, feelings, attitudes, and/or beliefs held in human consciousness. A woman has faith in the strength of her relationship with her spouse, and experiences no doubts when her spouse needs to travel for business.

4. **Conscious Faith from our True Identity, or Higher Self:** based on Divine Ideas, Laws, and Principles. We have Faith in the Spiritual Principles and use them to be the best person or Christ we can be.

Now that you have a better idea of the Power/Ability of Faith, we invite you to practice strengthening it in your own life experience, using the following Putting It Into Action Exercises for FAITH.

Faith ~ Putting It Into Practice

Faith ~ Activity One:

Complete the following sentences quickly, without giving a lot of thought to it:

Growing up, I was taught _____

When it comes to goal setting, I realize _____

The last time I affirmed success, _____

I feel like prayer is _____

When things do not go the way I expect, I _____

If I could have a "re-do" in some area of my life, _____

_____

When I think about God, I believe _____

The word "impossible" _____

Now that you have completed the sentences, read back through your responses, and identify underlying beliefs you have that affect the way you make life choices. Over the next week, become aware of how your beliefs are impacting your experience. In your journal, it might look like this:

Experience	Underlying Belief
I got upset when a store clerk was rude to me.	I always get treated badly by service people.
I was depressed because my favorite jeans were tight.	I'm never going to get into shape. I'm fat!
When I didn't get selected to give the presentation for the Executive Briefing, I took it personally.	I am unworthy. I don't deserve anything good. They wanted someone who looks more professional.

As you read through your "beliefs," apply this question: What would this belief look like if it came from my highest and best Christ Consciousness? Then practice using that new, revised belief and notice any outward changes in your experience. Your journal might continue:

Revised Belief from Christ Consciousness	New Experience
Everyone is Divine, including me. I deserve to be treated with respect, & I treat others with respect and love.	Clerk apologized and actually gave me a value-added!
I am beautiful ... I am Divine ...and I deserve to be fit and healthy.	I changed my diet and lost 5 pounds in two weeks! Jenny told me I looked radiant! Wow! I feel radiant!
I am worthy! I deserve the best.	I realized I needed to improve my skills in presentation. It is not personal.

Faith ~ Activity Two:

As you think about the specific area you want to work on through-out this course, **brainstorm a list of your beliefs related to this issue, up until now.** For example, if your area was wanting to learn to dance, beliefs up till now might include: I believe I am way too old to take dance lessons now; I've always been so clumsy; I am not flexible enough to be a dancer; I just don't have the body of a dancer.)

As you think about your selected area, **what specific beliefs do you need to develop?** Create specific denials and affirmations to support the revised beliefs. (Let's take a moment to clarify denials and affirmations, so we are all approaching it from the same viewpoint! Denials are not an attempt to deny the reality of an event in our lives, or even a feeling we might be having; rather, they are used to deny or release the power we have given an idea, thought, belief, or attitude. Every denial is followed by an affirmation, which is simply a statement of a Spiritual Truth as it relates to us. Affirmations are stated in the first person, and are stated in a positive way.)

For example:
I give no power to age affecting my ability to achieve my goals. I affirm my faith in infinite possibilities as I move forward and dance!

Repeat the denials and affirmations you have created five times (yes, five times!) each morning, and five times before retiring. Throughout the day, become consciously aware of any doubts that surface related to your ability to achieve your chosen issue, and immediately upon becom-ing aware of a doubt, stop! In that moment, repeat your denial and affir-mation five time (out loud, if possible ~ depending on where you are)!

Example: Healthy Eating

Throughout this book, we will have a specific example to help you understand how to complete the activity related to your selected area of improvement. For the purposes of the book, we will imagine that someone selected the goal of Healthy Eating as the area to improve. We will use Healthy Eating to demonstrate how to work with each power's "Putting It Into Action" activity. Here is the example for Faith, Activity Two:

Belief I have had up till now: I have believed I am a carbo-holic, and cannot handle any type of diet that requires a restriction on carb-related foods.

Belief I need to develop: I have faith in my ability to choose how much of any one food I eat, and I can manage to keep a healthy amount of carbohydrates in my diet.

Denial: I give no power to carbohydrates in my diet.
My new affirmation: I am in charge of what I eat, and I choose foods that are healthy, energizing, and delicious!)

Faith Affirmation:

*I claim Faith now. I believe I am the best person and
the best Christ I can be.*

If you have faith as small as a mustard seed, you can say to this mulberry tree, 'Be uprooted and planted in the sea,' and it will obey you.

~ Luke 17:6

Strength

Ability to endure, stay the course, last, be persistent, persevere, and be stable.

Color: Spring Green

Apostle: Andrew

Location: Small of the Back

I claim Strength now. Regardless of the circumstances, I stay the course so I can be the best Christ I can be.

Strength

Overview

- Apostle: Andrew
- Location: Small of the Back
- Color: Spring Green
- Linked with the Ability of Faith

STRENGTH is the ability to endure, stay the course, last, be persistent, persevere, and be stable.

From ego/personality: The ability to endure, stay the course, last, be persistent, persevere, and be stable based on our senses, thoughts, feelings and beliefs. We use STRENGTH to stick to a diet or a workout program. We can also use STRENGTH to be stubborn with a "don't confuse me with the facts" attitude.

- *Underdeveloped Strength* shows up as the inability to stick with a project or a goal. A person with underdeveloped Strength may flit from unfinished project to unfinished project.

- *Overdeveloped and/or unbalanced Strength* shows up as being stubborn, unduly forceful or perhaps obsessive compulsive. For example, a person with overdeveloped Strength might forge ahead with a plan, even though everyone else realizes the futility of it.

From elevated consciousness: The ability to endure, stay the course, last, be persistent, persevere, and be stable based on Ideas, Truths, Principles, and Laws that are Divine in nature. We use STRENGTH to be persistent in being the best person and/or Christ we can be.

*H*ave you ever gone to an amusement park and spied a ride you really wanted to go on? It looked so exciting, and yet, there was a level of fear that kept you from riding it. Then perhaps you began to have a conversation with yourself! Your intellect began by telling you, "Look, it's only a ride! It's got to be safe. Look at all those people coming off the ride laughing and having fun." Then you start feeling queasy and nervous, and your internal dialogue switches to, "STOP! DANGER! WHAT ARE YOU THINKING? You are going to get hurt or maybe even die if you go on that ride."

In a sense, you are carrying conflicting beliefs: one says it is safe and fun, while the other says it is not safe and you will surely get hurt. Finally you make the decision to get on the ride, and you get in line. As you wind through the line, you are still having the internal dialogue, increasingly using your Power/Ability of Strength. You use Strength to stay the course … maybe even endure ... with the decision to take the ride no matter how loud and stringent that "voice" for the belief that it is dangerous screams in your head. Finally, you use your strength to step onto the ride — and off you go on a fun-filled experience. And the cool part is that when you get off the ride, the first thing you'll say is, "Wow! I want to do that again!"

Let's explore another example of our Strength Power/Ability. Imagine you are in a position of authority with employees. You become aware of some behavior or performance that is not up to speed. You know you need to say something to this person, but are reluctant. Perhaps you are afraid the person will not like you anymore. You have a strong need to be liked, and yet, you know it is the right thing to do to speak up. Sometimes doing the right thing is not necessarily the easiest thing to do! After dealing with an internal struggle, you give yourself a good talking to, and pump up your Power/Ability of Strength to do what you must do, despite "the voice" that says you need to be liked.

Strength and Faith are connected. The more we really believe in something, the easier it is to support or sustain. It is harder to stand up for something we are lukewarm about, and nearly impossible when we do not really care at all. It is also difficult to stand firm when, like in the situations above, we have conflicting beliefs. We feel strongly both ways! In these cases, we must decide which belief we want to support, and then reinforce it by using our Strength Power/Ability, which impacts our thoughts, feelings and actions. As we do so, that belief will increasingly become the prominent one.

Strength is that innate ability by which we are able to endure, stay the course, last, be persistent, persevere, and be stable. A person can use brute physical strength to accomplish something like removing a stuck lid on a jar; in the same way, there is a brute mental strength we use to plow through a difficult project or handle a major emotional hit like the loss of a loved one. A person with underdeveloped Strength just can't stick with a project or a goal.

On the other hand, you probably know someone who has an overdeveloped and/or unbalanced Strength. You can tell because this person is stubborn, unduly forceful, or perhaps obsessive compulsive. Another common example of overdeveloped Strength in the sense realm is a person who hoards all sorts of things. S/he uses the power of strength to stay the course and hang onto stuff. People can hang on to things as well as erroneous thoughts, feelings, and beliefs. It is always good to keep in mind that when people are exhibiting any of these extreme kinds of behaviors, there is a belief fueling it. The person who cannot finish a project might truly believe they are unworthy, or have always been called a failure. The individual who hoards may really believe that there is not enough, and so they continue to add to their stockpile.

We've discussed some extreme examples of unbalanced Strength. So now, let's take a look at how we use Strength in our everyday lives, in a positive way. Here are a few examples of simple ways we use strength in our ordinary thoughts, feelings, and actions as we discern, interpret, and perceive situations:

- Imagine someone you respect (a person in authority or maybe even one of your parents) says you are irresponsible. You think, "That is not true." You put feeling into your belief that the statement is not true. You use Strength to speak up for yourself, in spite of what that person may think or do. You might respond, "That is not true.

I refuse to accept that label. I am a responsible person. I get up every morning, get to work on time, finish my projects on time and take care of my own needs and the needs of my love ones."

- A person shopping in a store is attracted to a beautiful, ornate wooden bird cage. As the person examines the cage more closely, s/he notices (through the senses of touch and sight) that the cage is fragile. Suddenly a piece breaks off. You probably can relate to their first response, which might be to look around to see if anyone noticed, quickly put the cage back on the shelf, and get as far from that cage as possible! But imagine that this person also has a strong belief in doing the right thing. By using the Power of Strength to overcome the child-like reaction, this person then tells a sales person what happened.

We also can use Strength in adverse ways based on beliefs derived from an erroneous interpretation or understanding of our thoughts, feelings, and what we are discerning, interpreting and perceiving through our senses. For example:

- Recall that in the last chapter on Faith we used the example of the person who had a strong belief that rats had no bones, because the rats could squeeze through such tight spaces. The person saw a rat … or maybe many rats … do this and came to this conclusion, this belief. And no matter what anybody said to the contrary, the belief was maintained ... and probably reinforced by defending it. The Ability of Strength is what was used to hold onto this belief.

- Remember the old Frank Sinatra song, "I Did It My Way?" While it made a great #1 hit on the music charts, in the real world a person who must do everything his or her own way is erroneously using the Ability of Strength. Imagine working with a colleague to finish a joint project. No matter how good your ideas are, your colleague simply has to have it his or her way. Unless one of you gives in, the project will never be completed! Of course, there are times when it is important to do things your way. But it is also important to be open to new ideas or different viewpoints. It means knowing when to employ your Ability of Strength... and when not to.

In each of these examples, Strength is engaged based on some belief held in sense consciousness. When we become aware of how we are already using Strength in our everyday lives, it becomes easier to know how to consciously apply Strength at ever higher levels of consciousness. As in the other applications of Strength, there is always a belief which supports that Strength.

For example, we can use the Ability of Strength to be the best Christ we can be. Or, if that goal seems too lofty at first, we can use it to be the best person we can be. Whether it be the best Christ we can be or the best person we can be, there must first be a belief that this is possible, even if at first it is simply the size of a mustard seed. As we use our Strength to reinforce that belief, it becomes easier and easier to believe the goal is possible. Ultimately, we are able to achieve the goal of being the best person or best Christ! As we go about the day, we use Strength to stay the course and persevere in being the best person or best Christ we can be. In the face of challenges or temptation to act from our personality or egos, we use Strength, buttressed from Faith, to continue being the best person or Christ we can be.

Let's look at Strength in another way. Strength (along with all the other Abilities) can be expressed from four different levels of consciousness:

1. **Unconscious Strength:** based on a cause in subconscious mind which consists of beliefs that are not in our moment to moment awareness. You might be strong, steadfast or even "bullheaded" without realizing it or really knowing why, because it is being fueled from some unconscious or subconscious belief.

2. **Conscious Strength from our senses:** based on something in physicality we are gleaning through our sight, sound, scent, touch, and/or taste. A person slips and takes a pretty bad fall on the ice. From that point on, this individual is steadfast about being very careful around icy sidewalks.

3. **Conscious Strength from our human personality:** based on thoughts, feelings, attitudes, and/or beliefs held in human consciousness. A person believes that s/he can become a doctor. So, this person does everything to stay on track to become a doctor, no matter what distractions or seeming obstacles come along.

4. **Conscious Strength from our True Identity, or Higher Self:** based upon Divine Ideas, Laws, and Principles. This is when we are not deterred, no matter what, from staying the course to be the best Christ we can be. We use Strength to overcome whatever temptations come along.

Strength: Putting It Into Practice

Strength — Activity One:

Part 1:

Think back to a situation in your past that feels incomplete: a lost opportunity; a decision you wish you could change; an activity or responsibility you left unfinished; etc.

- What were the reasons for the lack of completion?

- As you think back on the situation, what kind of internal conversation did you have with yourself?

- How were you using the power of Strength to sabotage your own success?

- What were the pay-offs to you to leave things incomplete or unsatisfactory?

Part 2:

Now, think back to a situation in your past where you were successful in achieving a goal: completing a course of study; learning a new skill; finishing a project; sealing a business deal; etc.

- What roadblocks did you encounter along the way, and how did you move through them?

- What kept you on track, inspired and motivated to see the situation through to a successful completion?

- How did you use the Power of Strength to stay the course and achieve success?

As you revisit these two life experiences, think about how you handled things differently. What lessons and tools can you identify that can help you more effectively use you Power/Ability of Strength to be successful? Can you identify the beliefs that were supporting your use of Strength in both situations?

Strength — Activity 2:

As you think about the specific area you want to work on throughout this course, brainstorm a list of potential barriers that could sabotage your success. Next to each one, identify Strength tools that can help you stay the course.

Example: Healthy Eating

Potential Barrier	Strength Tool
My mother bakes my favorite dessert, and I don't want to hurt her feelings, so I eat it.	Set boundaries with mother ahead of time ("I know you love to fix my favorite dessert, but I am really trying to stick to my new eating plan, and I'd really appreciate your help.")
	Claim I'm not hungry, and take some home with me for later (and don't eat it!)
	Take only a small piece, and plan my other eating around it.

Strength Affirmation:

I claim Strength now. Regardless of the circumstances, I stay the course so I can be the best person and the best Christ I can be.

Judgment/ Wisdom

Ability to judge, evaluate, discern, be wise, appraise, and apply what is known

Color: Yellow

Apostle: James son of Zebedee

Location: Pit of Stomach

I claim Wisdom now. I use Wisdom to wisely discern how to apply what I understand, so I am being the best Christ I can be.

Judgment is a faculty of the mind that can be exercised in two ways—from sense perception or spiritual understanding. If its action be based on sense perception, its conclusions are fallible and often condemnatory; if based on spiritual understanding, they are safe.

~ Charles Fillmore
Revealing Word, p. 113

Judgment/Wisdom

Overview

- Apostle: James son of Zebedee
- Location: Pit of Stomach
- Color: Yellow
- Linked with Love, Understanding, and Will

JUDGMENT/WISDOM is the ability to judge, evaluate, discern, be wise, appraise, and apply what is known.

From ego/personality: The ability to judge, evaluate, discern, be wise, appraise, and apply what is known based on our senses, thoughts, feelings, and beliefs. We use JUDGMENT to choose what we eat and wear. We also use JUDGMENT to be judgmental, discriminatory and shrewd.

- *Underdeveloped Judgment* results in a person who cannot make decisions, is indecisive, and perhaps cannot discern good from bad.

- *Overdeveloped Judgment* results in a person who is highly judgmental, discriminatory (as in being racist or sexist), and could even be shrewd. This person might also be overly picky about details, always finding fault with results.

From elevated consciousness: The ability to judge, evaluate, discern, be wise, appraise, and apply what is known based on Ideas, Truths, Principles and Laws that are Divine in nature. We use JUDGMENT to discern how to apply what we know in order to be the best person and/or Christ we can be.

*H*ave you ever been with a group of friends, preparing to have lunch together, and someone poses the question, "Where do you want to go to eat?" It becomes very frustrating when everyone responds with, "Oh, I don't care. Whatever everyone else wants to do is fine with me." It can lead to a long decision-making period, and a short lunch time! Even with such simple situations as this, we call on our Power/Ability of Judgment. Judgment gets a bad rap these days. We even use Jesus' own words to support our criticism of Judgment: "Do not judge, or you too will be judged" (Matthew 7:1, NIV). And yet, don't you think it's odd that Jesus would turn around and call the Pharisees and Sadducees vipers and hypocrites? Sounds like judging to us! And what about his attitude toward that poor little fig tree he cursed because it was not bearing fruit, even though it was not the season for the fruit to be ripe (Mark 11:12-14, 20-21).

And how about you? Have you ever been in a conversation when someone says, "Oh, but you're judging!" We sure have. And don't you wonder just what they think they are doing in that moment? Judging us! We humans sure are funny creatures!

Yes, judgment has gotten a bad rap. And, it does not have to be that way. It's true; we all have an innate Ability to Judge. We are judging machines (more about that in a bit). It is not the Ability of Judgment that is the problem; it is how we use it. We can certainly feel much better if we use some synonyms for the word judgment: wisdom, discernment, evaluation, or appraisal. And still, we are judging. And that can be a good thing!

Now, let's look at how we are judging machines. Our lives would be paralyzed into a numbing sameness if we did not constantly judge, evaluate, discern or appraise. In fact, we'd never get anything accomplished at all if we did not use our judgment. Have you ever been around someone who wants to get the best deal — so s/he keeps gathering data and evaluating information ad infinitum—and never makes a decision! Their Judgment Ability is on hold!

Everything we do is wrapped up in the Ability of Judgment. Think about it. You made a judgment about whether to purchase this book;

should I buy this book or not? The bottom line involved discerning whether it would be good for you to buy this book (we trust it is!). Once you purchased the book, another judgment is made about when and how much of the book you read.

Let's look at some other areas of our lives where we use Judgment:

- Each of us makes some sort of judgment about what time we get up in the morning. Sometimes we get up early, sometimes we sleep in. We base that decision on our assessment of the schedule for the day.

- What clothes are we going to wear? One day that blouse or shirt is the perfect one to wear; sometime later it just does not look right (we discerned we would not look appropriate in it for today's activities).

- We made a judgment about whether there's enough time to eat breakfast, and if there were, we made a judgment about what to eat.

- When we get to work, we use Judgment to discern what to do first and for how long.

Even though these may seem like inconsequential and insignificant evaluations, we are still using the Ability of Judgment. And just like all the Abilities, we can choose to use our Ability of Judgment in ways that are more detrimental to our consciousness:

- Someone cuts us off on the way to work. "You jerk!" we think to ourselves, or worse, say it out loud.

- We forget to pick up the gallon of milk on the way home and think, "Dad-gummit, I forgot the milk! I'm so forgetful!" Or worse, "I'm so stupid" or, "I'm _____", you fill in the blank!

- Have you ever been engaged in a boss or employer bashing conversation? Think of all the judgments that happen in those discussions. Whew!

- Here's a great example: Two friends were driving down the highway on a very cold fall day, after purchasing some birds that needed to be kept warm. They suddenly realized that the power to the brooder was off! One friend commented, "Look at us — Two dummies!" The friend simply and quietly responded, "One not so smart — and one dummy!" Now, can we say JUDGMENT??!!

Using Judgment at the lower, more ego-centric level, can backfire on us. It reminds us of that old saying, "When I have one finger pointing at you, I have three pointing at me." Thoughts held with feeling in mind produce after their kind; negative judgments of others that are in my mind affect my mind. We constantly slander and slur ourselves when we do this. In a way, these are negative affirmations. Perhaps we should call them defamations. (Hey, that was pretty smart! Oops — There's another statement based on judgment. See, we told you that we are judging machines!)

What to do? The solution is to become truly conscious in this now moment about how we are using the Ability of Judgment/Wisdom. Awareness and self-knowledge go a long way to the raising of consciousness. The key to the successful use of the Ability of Judgment/Wisdom is to get it under our wise control. We simply have been going about our lives blithely judging this, evaluating that, discerning this and appraising something else. Sometimes our judgments are useful and good for our consciousness; other times, not so good. (Did you catch the judgment that happened just then? Was it good or bad? Hmmm?)

First of all, get over it. We cannot not use Judgment/ Wisdom; they are always at work. And that can be a good thing ... or not. Let's begin to explore Judgment/Wisdom to demonstrate how we can use this Ability more consciously and thus, more effectively.

In a broad and general way, life boils down to a series of judgments:

1. First you make a judgment about whether you want something in your life. The underlying decision is basically reduced to asking yourself: "Is it good for me or bad for me? Do I want it or not?"
2. If you want it in your life (it is good for you), another judgment is made by asking yourself: "Who is going to get it for me or make sure it happens?" You could get it on your own, work with someone else to get it, or convince someone else to get it for you.

3. Or, if you determine you do not want it in your life (it is bad for you), another judgment is made by asking yourself: "Who is going to remove it from my life?" You could remove it, work with someone else to remove it, or convince someone else to remove it for you.

Let's look at an example. Suppose you are working in your home office on a Saturday, and you notice you are hungry.

1. You want a sandwich. In other words, you have judged that a sandwich would be good for you.

2. You are thinking, "I'm pretty busy, it would be great if my partner got it for me." You call out, "Honey, are you hungry? I sure would like a sandwich." In other words, you have made the judgment that you do not want to make the sandwich yourself, so you are subtly trying to convince your partner to fix it for you.

Here's another example:

1. You notice that the garbage can is flowing over in the kitchen. The judgment is that it is bad to have an overflowing garbage can in the kitchen. You do not want it.

2. You decide to take the garbage out yourself. In the other words, you decide that it is good for you to take out the garbage.

Judgment/Wisdom is the innate ability by which we judge, evaluate, discern, use wisdom, appraise, and apply what is known. How we wisely evaluate, discern, appraise and apply what is known is what we base our decisions on. The actual choosing or deciding uses the Ability of Will ... more on that when we get to that chapter!

An underdeveloped Ability of Judgment results in a person who has a crippled ability to evaluate anything. This person is wishy-washy, somewhat unpredictable, and perhaps lacks standards by which to discern or judge. This person could also be indecisive, lacking the Judgment necessary to support the Ability of Will ... like a leaf blowing in the wind.

On the other hand, over-developed Judgment/Wisdom comes across as judgmental, perhaps erroneously discriminatory, condemnatory or shrewd in a negative way. If we want to use the Ability of Judgment/Wisdom in the most productive ways, we really must use It in conjunction with Love and Understanding.

Let's make this really practical by taking a sensible look at how we use Judgment in our everyday lives. Sometimes we use Judgment in a positive way based on our ordinary thoughts, feelings, and what we are discerning, interpreting, and perceiving through our senses.

Here are a few illustrations:

- A perfect example is flossing! We all know the infamous dental adage: only floss the teeth you want to keep! When you go to the dentist's office, we can guarantee you will get a reminder about the proper technique to use when flossing, along with a not-so-subtle reminder about how often to do it. You will probably even get a little case of dental floss along with your complimentary tooth-brush and your bill! Now you have the Understanding about what to do, but up to this point, you are only borrowing the Wisdom/Judgment of the dentist. As you make the decision to actually practice flossing on a regular basis (which is Will — more on that in a later chapter), you notice how much fresher and cleaner your teeth feel. Then, on your next dental visit, you realize how much easier the cleaning is, and you receive kudos from the dental hygienist and your dentist. Now you have the Wisdom to continue making regular flossing part of your daily routine.

- We notice over time that foods containing certain ingredients cause heartburn (definitely a sense thing!). We would then use our Ability of Judgment to apply what we know and discern what foods to eat and what foods not to eat.

We also can use Judgment in adverse ways based on beliefs derived from an erroneous interpretation or understanding of our thoughts, feelings, and what we are discerning and evaluating through our senses. Some examples:

- In the illustration of the person who used the sense of sight to see a rat squeezing through a small hole, judgment was used to decide that the rat had no bones.

- A man notices that he gets a cold when he is out in a cold rain. He then uses his Ability of Judgment/Wisdom erroneously to come to the conclusion that being wet and cold causes colds. He then applies the same Ability of Judgment every time it rains to stay out of the rain.

While all of these examples certainly demonstrate some of the ways we use the Ability of Judgment in our lives, they do not give any indication of the best and highest way to use this important Ability. In all of the forgoing examples, Judgment is engaged based on what we are discerning and surmising from sense consciousness. Awareness of how we are already using the Ability of Judgment in our everyday lives helps us to know how to use It at ever higher levels of consciousness. The highest and best use of this Ability is to evaluate and discern, moment by moment, how effectively we are being the best person and the best Christ we can be. We can also use this Ability to see beyond the appearance of another person's personality/ego, attitudes, and actions, to discern the presence of this beautiful Christ Nature. Further, this Ability is used to apply what we know about Divine Ideas, Laws, and Principles. We use this Ability to make them ever more practical.

Here's another way to look at Judgment. It (along with all the other Abilities) can be expressed from different levels of consciousness:

1. **Unconscious Judgment:** based on a cause in subconscious mind which consists of beliefs that are not in our moment to moment awareness. An example is when we have a reaction to a person or a situation without being aware of a conscious, cognitive process.

2. **Conscious Judgment from our senses:** based on something in physicality we are gleaning through our sight, sound, scent, touch, and/or taste. We eat luscious dark chocolate. We love the taste. So, nearly every time we see dark chocolate, we judge that it would be good to have some ... and do!

3. **Conscious Judgment from our human personality:** based on thoughts, feelings, attitudes, and/or beliefs held in human consciousness. A person holds the belief that s/he will become a minister. S/he would then use the Ability of Judgment to make wise decisions on what courses to take to prepare for the ministry.

4. **Conscious Judgment from our True Identity, or Higher Self:** based upon Divine Ideas, Laws, and Principles. Judgment would be used to evaluate how we are doing moment to moment, discerning the thoughts and actions that would demonstrate being the best Christ we can be.

Judgment/Wisdom: Putting It Into Practice

Judgment — Activity One:

Without thinking, jot down your immediate responses to each of the following statements:

Behaviors I find irritating, inappropriate, or offensive are:

Five attitudes or beliefs I really value are:

The best way to convince me of something is:

I base my decisions on:

When I'm not sure what to do, my "modus operandi" is:

Reflect on your responses, and see what they tell you about the ways you make judgments in your daily life. What is working for you? What would you like to change?

Judgment — Activity Two:

As you think about the specific area you want to work on throughout this course, brainstorm a list of judgments you have made related to this area. Then ask yourself the following three questions, and reflect on the answers that arise:

- Is this really true?
- How is this judgment serving me?
- What additional information do I need to be able to use my Judgment Power/Ability at a more elevated level of Consciousness?

Example: Healthy Eating

Judgment: Carbohydrates are my enemy! Therefore, I should eliminate them from my diet.

Is this really true? Well, probably not. Carbohydrates provide energy power, but they also turn to sugar quickly, and in excess can pack on pounds. By totally eliminating carbs I could be robbing myself of necessary energy food.

How is this judgment serving me? It helps me get sympathy from others ("Poor me! No carbs in my diet!") Hmmm... Is it sympathy I want? I am playing the role of victim, and sabotaging my own success!

What additional information do I need to be able to use my Judgment Power/Ability at a more elevated level of Consciousness? I need to gather good, sound medical information about the value of carbs, and how to add them to my diet in a healthy way. I can also create a check-list of criteria to use to evaluate food with carbs, to be able to discern which ones are YES foods, and which ones I should avoid.

Judgment/Wisdom Affirmation:

I claim Wisdom and Elevated Judgment now. I use Judgment to wisely discern how to apply what I understand, so I can be the best person and the best Christ I can be.

Love

Ability to feel affection for, desire, attract oneself to, harmonize, and unify.

Color: Pink

Apostle: John

Location: Back of the Heart

I claim Love now. I use Love to attract myself to what is highest and most spiritual, so I can be the best Christ I can be.

Love, in Divine Mind, is the idea of universal unity. In expression, it is the power that joins and binds together the universe and everything in it. Love is a harmonizing, constructive power. When it is made active in consciousness, it conserves substance and reconstructs, rebuilds, and restores [us] and [our] world.

~ Charles Fillmore
Keep a True Lent, p. 151

Love

Overview

- Apostle: John
- Location: Back of the Heart
- Color: Pink
- Linked with Wisdom and Understanding

LOVE is the ability to feel affection for, desire, attract oneself to, harmonize, and unify.

From ego/personality: The ability to feel affection for, desire, attract oneself to, harmonize, and unify based on our senses, thoughts, feelings, and beliefs. We can use LOVE to be loving or lustful. Through our desire we can use LOVE to bring good or bad into our lives based on what we are focused upon.

- *Underdeveloped Love* results in a person who has a limited ability to feel affection or positive regard for another person. It can also result in a person who has little desire.

- *Overdeveloped Love* results in a person who "loves indiscriminately" or inappropriately. It may also show up as a kind of fatal attraction, neediness, or lust.

From elevated consciousness: The ability to feel affection for, desire, attract oneself to, harmonize, and unify based on Ideas, Truths, Principles and Laws that are Divine in nature. We use LOVE to desire Christ Nature so that we harmonize everything in our life to be the best person and/or Christ we can be.

*T*hink about the incredible number of ways we use the word "Love" — as diverse as "I love my soul mate" to "I love that new song" to "I love chocolate-chip cookie dough ice cream!" It is the same word, but obviously has different intents.

Perhaps one of the most famous phrases from the Bible comes from 1 John 16, which simply says "God is love." In fact, the same scripture informs us that those who abide in love abide in God and God abides in them. We are encouraged to love our neighbors as ourselves. And, at the same time, we must realize that God, Divine Mind, is so much more than love. Love is simply one aspect among many.

When we speak of the Power or Ability of Love, we can really define it as three potential aspects:

- Emotion: the ability to feel affection for, or desire something;

- Attraction: the ability to attract ourselves toward something; and

- Harmony: the ability to unify or bring agreement and accord to our thoughts or to a situation.

Let's explore these a little more deeply. The **Emotion**, or feeling side of love (to feel affection for, or desire something) is probably one of the most written about, talked about, and sought after experiences. It is defined as a deep, fervent affection for another person. It is associated with a warm affection and high regard for another person, be it parent, partner, child, or friend. While some people may not be too good at expressing love, they still have some understanding of it and want it. While we wax elegantly about the positive aspects of this kind of love, we tend to overlook the darker side, which can show up as lust, abuse, or other distorted forms.

The second aspect of the Ability of Love is the **Attraction** side (the ability to attract ourselves toward something). This is the Ability we use to desire another person or thing. We are sure you can easily see it is not entirely separate from the feeling side. The Attraction or thinking side of Love is demonstrated in phrases like, "I love chocolate" or "plants love sunlight." It is the Ability to attract oneself to something that is desired, wanted, needed, or required. It is the primary Ability behind what is called the Law of Attraction.

Okay — since it has come up, let's address the Law of Attraction so we are all on the same page. It is often taught that we attract people, situations, and things to us. We believe it is more like we attract ourselves to people, situations, and things. For example, when you decide to buy something like a Volkswagen Beetle, you will suddenly begin seeing more of them as you drive around. It is obvious that there is not a Universe (aka God) putting more Volkswagens on the road for you to see; they are not coming to you like a magnet attracts iron filings. No, it is actually your decision and desire you use to attract yourself to the Volkswagens. They have been there all along. You are now "sorting" the incoming visual data based on your decision and desire. The ability to desire is fired by the Ability of Love.

This works whether the desire is positive or negative. For example, an alcoholic does not attract a co-dependent partner; rather. the alcoholic attracts himself or herself to the co-dependent person... and vice versa.

The third aspect of the Ability of Love is **Harmony** – the ability to harmonize or unify (to bring into harmony, accord, or agreement [dictionary.reference.com]). A singer harmonizes with another singer; strings on a violin are harmonized with each other. We can create mighty good results through using the Ability of Love to harmonize and unify, when we bring harmony between conflicting positions, people, or countries. Most of us have a tendency to view these two processes purely from the positive or good side; however, we must be wise and discern (using the Power/Ability of Judgment) that this is only half the truth.

However, while the Ability of Love is neutral in character, it's impact can be either positive or negative, depending on how it is applied. Its use is determined by the consciousness of the individual. We must be wise and realize that we can desire, want, need, or seem to require people and things that are not really good for us. While it may sound odd, remember, it is our Love Ability that powers what we desire in the moment ... the good, the bad and the ugly! It harmonizes everything to match what we are desiring. So unless we set a clear intention to control our Power/Ability of Love, we may end up harmonizing with inappropriate people, ideas, or things.

Think about it. When we are angry, aren't we, in an odd way, desiring and wanting to be angry in that moment? Don't we then tend to filter and therefore harmonize and unify nearly everything to match that anger? What if we are depressed or feeling sad? Once again, it does sound strange and more than a little odd to say that we desire or want to feel depressed or sad. And, yet, this is still the case, since this is what we are deciding in the moment. That is not to say there is not a "good reason" to feel sad or depressed. We simply want to convey that this is what we are choosing in the moment, even if it is driven from a subconscious level. If a person is "desiring or wanting" to feel sad or depressed, then the Ability of Love is also harmonizing and unifying everything else to match the sadness and depression. That's where the phrase "Misery loves company" comes from (and we would actually say, misery loves miserable company!) So, we each want to be vigilant about what we are desiring, wanting, needing, or requiring in the moment because the Ability of Love is activated, and it will harmonize and unify to "match" whatever we are desiring, wanting, needing or requiring.

When it is said that Love is like a mighty magnet the assumption is that Love attracts. In truth, it is like a magnet through which we attract ourselves to what we desire, want, need, or require. Not only is this the Power behind the Law of Attraction, it is also the Power behind the Law of Mind Action, which says "thoughts held in mind produce after their kind." This means the thoughts we are holding in the moment are the thoughts we are desiring or wanting through the Ability of Love, and this same Ability will also tend to harmonize and unify our thoughts to match the thoughts we are holding.

Since the Ability of Love is the ability to desire or want, It can also be viewed as the ability to focus and intend. What we desire or want, we tend to focus upon. What we desire, we intend to have. Much has been written about the power of intention and basically it is "an act or instance of determining mentally upon some action or result, the end or object intended" (dictionary.reference.com). It is said that what we focus on increases. What we focus on, intend, or desire is what we are "loving" or love in the moment. While it may seem weird, it is true that when we focus on the "negative" we actually "love" the negative in the moment. It is by this focus (the Ability of Love) that we attract ourselves to more of the same negativity as well as harmonize and unify our thoughts, matching them with that negative thought. We now tend to see things more and more through this negative focus, which then tends to "out-picture" in the outer/exterior realm.

You see, we have been limiting our definitions by only seeing them in the "good" sense, since in the Absolute there is only "Absolute Good." In so doing, we have missed a very important point that, when we fully realize its import, will re-establish our power and control over our consciousness and our lives. Charles Fillmore wrote that each of the Powers can be used on the personal level instead of the universal level. We think of the words like harmony, harmonizer, love, and desire in a positive sense. Bringing harmony to a situation typically means smoothing things out and making everything better. However, if Love/Harmony is a PRIN-CIPLE, then It does not care how It is used. Love, the great harmonizer, really is a principle that brings two or more things into harmony with each other. It says nothing about what the quality is of the things being harmonized. It says nothing about what that harmony looks or feels like. So, when we are focusing on the negative, we could say we are loving the negative. Then this principle simply harmonizes thoughts and feelings to match the negative we are focusing upon. This obviously affects our consciousness in the same way, and there will be a tendency to harmonize the outer with the same negative focus.

It may be relatively easy for us to love one another and for some, less so, to love oneself. However, it is both helpful and refreshing to know that we are forever equipped with the Ability of Love. It is not a matter of obtaining it; it is more a matter of figuring out how to use it … wisely. For this reason, the Ability of Love is often linked with the Ability of Judgment/Wisdom which, in turn, is linked with Understanding (the ability to know).

Love loves indiscriminately. It is important to be vigilant about how we are using the principle/thinking side of Love and the effect this has on our consciousness. We must become aware, moment to moment, what we are thinking and feeling because, through the Power/Ability of Love, this is what we will be increasing in consciousness. We must use Wisdom with Love so that we choose rightly.

Here's another way to look at Love. It (along with all the other Abilities) can be expressed from different levels of consciousness:

1. **Unconscious Love:** based on a cause in subconscious mind which consists of beliefs that are not in our moment to moment awareness. Now, this may seem strange; however, these would be desires and wants driven from subconscious/unconscious beliefs. We believe this is what the apostle Paul was referring to when he wrote about doing that which he did not want to do (Romans 7:19). When it seems an alcoholic is unconsciously attracting himself to a co-dependent, he probably "unconsciously reads" a batch of "signals or behavior cues" that a co-dependent is exhibiting.

2. **Conscious Love from our senses:** based on something in physicality we are gleaning through our sight, sound, scent, touch, and/or taste. For example, once having tasted a peppermint mocha latté, we might find ourselves desiring and attracting ourselves to that particular coffee treat. Walking through the mall, our senses inform us of a specialty coffee shop up ahead. Our desire for a peppermint mocha latté kicks in and voilá, we attracted ourselves to the coffee shop.

3. **Conscious Love from our human personality:** based on thoughts, feelings, attitudes, and/or beliefs held in human consciousness. For example, this occurs when we are aware of a belief that we want a partner who enjoys the same movies we do. Then we would use the Ability of Love to desire that particular trait as a requirement for someone we choose to spend time with. We would then attract ourselves to a person that likes the same movies we do.

4. **Conscious Love from our True Identity, or Higher Self:** based upon Divine Ideas, Laws, and Principles. This would result in the desire to be this True Identity, Christ. And, as a result, we would attract ourselves to behaviors, attitudes and feelings that we believe would support this True Identity, and help us to be the best person or Christ we could be.

Love: Putting It Into Practice

Love — Activity One:

A popular Bible verse concerning love comes from Matthew 5:44: "I tell you: Love your enemies and pray for those who persecute you." And in Matthew 22:37-39, Jesus said, "Thou shalt love the Lord thy God with all thy heart, and with all thy soul, and with all thy mind. This is the first and great commandment. And the second is like unto it, Thou shalt love thy neighbor as thyself."

Keeping these powerful verses in mind, identify specific ways you have demonstrated Love for each of the statements below:

1. Love your neighbor:

2. Love yourself:

3. Love your enemies:

4. Love God:

As you reflect on your responses, see what patterns you can identify. How are you using your Power/Ability to Love ... and what conscious decisions can you make so you can use Love from a higher level of consciousness?

Love — Activity 2:

As you think about the specific area you want to work on throughout this course, make a list of what you have attracted yourself to that is either helping or hindering your success. Become aware of what you focused on that contributed to attracting yourself to those particular things. What can you do differently, to use your Power/Ability of Love more effectively?

Example: Healthy Eating

Helping Me:

I reconnected with an old friend who had just released a book entitled, Healthy Living Cookbook. She gave me a copy and pointed out some of her favorite recipes. These recipes helped me change my eating habits.

How? I realized all my recipes were based on fatty, "comfort" foods, and that led me to be on the lookout for new recipes. While surfing the web, I attracted myself to a *Healthy Living Cookbook* because I noticed it was written by an old friend. I sent her an email which reconnected us.

Hindering Me:

I find myself at fast food restaurants way too often, tempted by the burger and fries that I love.

How? I am still holding thoughts about how much I miss my burger and fries. My thoughts then generate feeling like a martyr. That harmonizes with the thought and feeling of "poor me, I deserve a special treat. Look out burger and fries, here I come!"

How to use my Love Ability more effectively: Create some affirmations about deserving a healthy, fit, fully-functioning body. Post pictures of my head pasted on a great body, to reinforce why I want to do this. Maybe I could even create a picture of what the fat contained in an order of burger and fries actually looks like! YUK!

Love Affirmation:

I claim Love now. I use Love to attract myself to what is highest and most spiritual, so I can be the best person and the best Christ I can be.

Love is patient; love is kind. It is not envious or boastful or arrogant or rude. It does not insist on its own way; it is not irritable or resentful; it does not rejoice in wrongdoing, but rejoices in the truth. It bears all things, believes all things, hopes all things, endures all things. Love never ends.

~ I Corinthians 13:4-8

Power/ Dominion

Ability to master, dominate, and control base senses, thoughts, feelings, and beliefs.

Color: Purple

Apostle: Phillip

Location: Throat, back of tongue, voicebox

I claim Dominion now. I use Dominion to master Divine Ideas so I can be the best Christ I can be.

ower, we must understand, is not an end in itself, not a goal to be sought. Rather, it is simply a means that enables us to attain the end of bringing forth God ideas on earth ... It is to be exercised not for the purpose of controlling others, but for the purpose of taking dominion over our own thoughts and feelings in order to come into a greater God awareness.

~ Winnifred Wilkinson Hausmann
Your God-Given Potential, p. 95

Power/Dominion

Overview

- Apostle: Phillip
- Location: The throat, back of tongue, voice box
- Color: Purple

POWER/DOMINION is the ability to master, dominate and control.

From ego/personality: The ability to master, dominate, and control based on our senses, thoughts, feelings, and beliefs. We use DOMINION to master a new concept or idea. We can also use DOMINION to control our thoughts and feelings. Or, we can use It to be domineering and controlling.

- *Underdeveloped Power/Dominion* results in a person who cannot master much. This person has little grasp of many ideas and concepts. This person has no sense of control in his/her life.

- *Overdeveloped Power/Dominion* results in a person who masters new ideas and concepts easily, and expects everyone else to be able to do so as well. This person probably is overly controlling about his or her own life and the lives of others, and can come across as very vocal and domineering.

From elevated consciousness: The ability to master, dominate, and control based on Ideas, Truths, Principles, and Laws that are Divine in nature. We use DOMINION to master the Divine Ideas that make it possible for us to be the best person and/or Christ we can be.

The Ability/Power of Power always sounds redundant and a bit confusing. In addition, in today's language, the term "power" gets a bad rap much like the term "judgment" does. It is usually associated with being "power hungry" or controlling of others in negative ways. In fact, a person who has the Power of Power overdeveloped is often seen as calculating or domineering. It is also important to emphasize that there are situations where having dominion and control over others is important and appropriate. A good example would be in raising children, where a family might be thought of as a kind of benevolent dictatorship. Equally, an adult child might have to take control of his or her parent's finances. Whatever the situation, it is best to have the healthy Abilities of Wisdom, Love, and Understanding working with the Power of Power/Dominion in order to ensure you are using it to Its highest and best capacity.

Since the phrase Power of Power is redundant and it is certainly open to getting a bad rap, it helps to realize the terms "dominion" and "mastery" actually come closer to the original intention. We can easily substitute the titles Ability/Power of Dominion or the Ability/Power of Mastery for the Power of Power, to create more clarity. Further, it is helpful to distinguish between the Ability of Strength and the Ability of Power/Dominion. Strength, you'll remember, is our ability to hold onto a thought or idea, to stay the course, and to be persistent. Power is the ability to master or have dominion over those thoughts or ideas. It is easy to see how we employ Strength in order to be persistent and stay the course until we master an idea or concept.

It is important to remember that all the Abilities have their greatest hope and capacity when used to raise one's own consciousness; they equally have usefulness in our relative, physical realm. While it is true that this Ability, as with all, can be misused, it is best to put our emphasis on its brighter, more positive side. Power-Dominion-Mastery has a dual function. We use it to master and have dominion over new ideas and concepts … especially Divine Ideas, Truths, and Principles. However, it is also the Ability by which we have control and dominion over unwanted thoughts, feelings, and beliefs that may interfere and impede our ability to master those ideas.

Here are a couple of simple examples:

- If we believe it is difficult to learn geometry, we would use the Ability of Power-Dominion-Mastery to have dominion over the belief that it is difficult to learn geometry. We would also be using this Ability to master the concepts of geometry.

- Similarly, we would use this Ability to master being the best Christ or person we can be, while using it to have dominion over and control of our personality/ego.

Here is one more case in point to illustrate how we use our Ability of Dominion. Every time we speak, we charge our words with energy. The character of that energetic charge is determined by the consciousness of the individual. Just listen to a person, and within moments you have a good idea of what consciousness they are coming from.

We exercise Dominion through our speech, and there are many ways to use it: denials, affirmations, prayer, praise, and thanksgiving. Let's go back to the idea that the Ability of Dominion is associated with Purple, Philip, Power – 3 P's — and translate them into 3 P's to define how we can use Dominion to its fullest benefit: Positive, Passionate, and Proactive!

- *POSITIVE* = What we say

- *PASSIONATE* = How we say it

- *PROACTIVE* = our expectations and the expansiveness of our words.

You have the power to create the appearance of monsters or miracles! When you seek, through meditation and prayer, to let the Christ instead of personal ego guide, govern, and direct your thoughts and feelings, a charge of spiritual energy is infused in your words. Jesus understood the power of the spoken word: In Matthew 12:37, He said, "For by thy words thou shalt be justified, and by thy words thou shalt be condemned."

Let's now review how the Ability of Dominion/Power is used at various levels of consciousness:

1. **Unconscious Dominion/Power:** based on a cause in subconscious mind which consists of beliefs that are not in our moment to moment awareness. This person would tend to be controlling in situations where unconscious beliefs are somehow activated or triggered. A person who has a subconscious low self-esteem belief would tend to control situations in a way that this belief is confirmed and reinforced. Alternatively, this person may be over-controlling to unconsciously compensate for low self-esteem.

2. **Conscious Dominion/Power from our senses:** based on something in physicality we are gleaning through our sight, sound, scent, touch, and/or taste. A young man watching other people snowboarding captures the fun and excitement of the sport. He gets excited, and decides he wants to learn how. So, through the use of the Ability of Dominion/Power, he is able to master the techniques needed to snowboard, while at the same time using the Ability of Dominion to dominate and control any fears and concerns he may have.

3. **Conscious Dominion/Power from our human personality:** based on thoughts, feelings, attitudes, and/or beliefs held in human consciousness. A young woman decides she wants to follow in the footsteps of her parents, to become a doctor. So, she must master all that is required to become a doctor. She would also use her Ability of Dominion to master and control any thoughts from her ego/personality that she does not have what it takes to become a doctor.

4. **Conscious Dominion/Power from our True Identity, or Higher Self:** based upon Divine Ideas, Laws, and Principles. A person who desires to be the best Christ s/he can be will have to master the concepts, Principles, and Divine Ideas involved in being the best Christ s/he can be. This person would also have to control any thoughts to the contrary arising from the personality/ego.

Power/Dominion: Putting It Into Practice

Power/Dominion — Activity One:

Make a list of the skills you possess.

Now make a list of your favorite hobbies, activities, and interests.

As you look back over these two lists, think about what went into making these skills, hobbies, activities, and interests viable in your everyday life. How do your skills interact with your hobbies, activities, and interests? (For example, do you have a skill in playing the piano, and an activity playing for your church choir?)

What steps did you take to gain dominion over the particular skills, hobbies, activities, or interests you have?

How can this help you in the future?

Power/Dominion — Activity Two:

As you think about the specific area you want to work on throughout this course, identify thoughts or beliefs you have that may be interfering with your success. How can you use the Ability of Power/Dominion to deal with those testy thoughts and beliefs?

Now make a list of the skills you must master in order to be successful in the area of your choice. How can you use the Ability of Power/Dominion to help you?

Example: Healthy Eating

Thoughts and Beliefs:

- I don't have the time to cook healthy food.

- I have never been successful at this before – why should this time be any different?

I can use Dominion to take control of the thoughts running amuck through my head. I can create powerful denial and affirmation statements to use whenever I become aware of these defeating statements in my consciousness.

Skills to master:

- How to prepare quick but healthy meals.

I can use Dominion to master my ability to cook healthy meals that are fast and easy to prepare.

Power/Dominion Affirmation:

I claim Dominion now. I use Dominion to master Divine Ideas so I can be the best person and the best Christ I can be.

Ability to visualize, conceptualize, and envision.

Color: Light Blue

Apostle: Bartholomew

Location: Between the eyes

I claim Imagination now. I visualize and imagine how to be the best Christ I can be.

When the faculties of mind are understood in their threefold relation – spirit, soul, body – it will be found that every form and shape originated in the imagination. It is through the imagination that the formless takes form.

~ Charles Fillmore
The Twelve Powers of Man, p. 71

Imagination

Overview

- Apostle: Bartholomew
- Location: Between the eyes
- Color: Light Blue

IMAGINATION is the ability to visualize, conceptualize, and envision.

From ego/personality: The ability to visualize, conceptualize, and envision based on our senses, thoughts, feelings, and beliefs. We use IMAGINATION to visualize a beautiful garden or to visualize how the boogeyman looks.

- *Underdeveloped Imagination* results in people who have little ability to visualize or picture anything that is not concrete and visible. They have difficulty conceptualizing an idea. For example, when looking for a new home, a person with underdeveloped Imagination would have difficulty visualizing what their furniture would look like in the places they view. Further, they cannot "see beyond" the appearance of the house. They could not visualize how the living room would look without the hot pink carpeting or purple passion paint on the walls, and therefore decide not to buy the house — even though it may be exactly what they need and want in terms of features and function.

- *Overdeveloped Imagination* results in people who may be excessive daydreamers, who spend so much time daydreaming that little or nothing is accomplished. It can also result in obsessive worrying, even advancing to the point of being delusional. A hypochondriac would be a good example of someone with an overdeveloped Ability of Imagination.

From elevated consciousness: The ability to visualize, conceptualize, and envision based on Ideas, Truths, Principles, and Laws that are Divine in nature. We use IMAGINATION to envision ourselves being the best person and/or Christ we can be.

*W*hen you were younger, did you ever lie back on the cool grass with a trusted friend on a hot summer day, enjoying the gentle breeze of summer caressing your face? Did you look up at the clouds and daydream? As you both looked up at the clouds, what did you see? Did you see more than clouds? Perhaps you saw a face in the clouds, an animal, or even an entire scene. If you had this kind of experience, you were using your Ability of Imagination. As you read this, you may have even been experiencing it again right now. If so, you are using your Ability of Imagination. Our oldest ancestors looked up at the stars and imagined seeing lions, water bearers, scorpions, and twins. They were using the Ability of Imagination. Children at Christmas time imagine a jolly old elf delivering Christmas presents, and have no trouble imagining him going to each and every home in a single night, let alone getting down the chimney! They are using their Ability of Imagination.

The Ability of Imagination is probably one of the most easily understood Powers/Abilities. Most of us have heard of the "screen of our minds" where we visualize what we want to create, need, or desire. It is easy to see how we use this Ability when we imagine the work we want to do, how we want to decorate our homes, or how a project will turn out. Some of us use the "screen of our minds" to picture how to get from point A to point B. Visionaries use this faculty well, especially if they can move their visions from consciousness to the physical realm.

A young girl may desire to make her own clothes. She daydreams and visualizes herself at the sewing machine making them. As she learns how to sew, she also learns how to make patterns. Soon, using her Ability of Imagination, she starts visualizing clothes of her own design and proceeds to make them.

Like all the Abilities, Imagination can be used in positive, uplifting ways or in negative, non-productive ways. Imagination is what powers worry. Mothers and fathers use the Ability of Imagination to worry about what might happen to their children. Or, they may worry about losing jobs or becoming ill. A child may imagine a boogeyman under the bed.

In the chapter on Faith, we shared the true story of a little boy who lived where there was a detached garage located a long distance from the safety and comfort of his home. He believed there was a man in the garage waiting to grab him in the dark and take him away. Every night the young boy would have to put his bike away in the garage. Every night he believed and visualized that there was a man waiting in the dark garage to grab him. He was very afraid. And, yet, no matter how many times he put that bike in the garage no one ever grabbed him. Still, through the Ability of his Imagination linked with his Ability of Faith the boy visualized and believed that a man was going to grab him.

Obviously, Imagination, like all the Abilities, does not stand alone. It is easy to see that Imagination is linked to Faith. We can also link it to Wisdom and Understanding, since we want to wisely know how and for what to use our Imagination. We can also link it to Love, because we tend to imagine and visualize what we desire, want, need, or require. We can even use imagination to visualize and picture our ideal partner, the person we want to love and be with.

Let's take a look at the use of the Ability of Imagination at the four levels of consciousness we have been exploring:

1. **Unconscious Imagination:** based on a cause in subconscious mind which consists of beliefs that are not in our moment to moment awareness. A person could be holding a subconscious belief that s/he is not intelligent. And, so, this person then imagines himself or herself as not intelligent. A painter might have a strong mental impression, totally unaware of the belief fueling it; then the painter begins to put paint to canvas based on what is being visualized in the mind.

2. **Conscious Imagination from our senses:** based on something in physicality we are gleaning through our sight, sound, scent, touch, and/or taste. This is when we see something we like in the outer world, like granite counter tops at a friend's home, and then visualize them in our own home. Or, when we are shopping for a new home, we visualize our furniture in it.

3. **Conscious Imagination from our human personality:** based on thoughts, feelings, attitudes and/or beliefs held in human consciousness. When a person sets an intention to become a writer, s/he begins to imagine and even daydream about creating a best-selling book.

4. **Conscious Imagination from our True Identity, or Higher Self:** based upon Divine Ideas, Laws, and Principles. This is when we visualize and conceptualize what it is like to be Christ, so we can be the best Christ we can be.

Imagination: Putting It Into Practice

Imagination — Activity One:

Choose *at least three* from the "Baker's Dozen" idea list below, to strengthen your Imagination Ability in a very practical way. Capture your experiences and thoughts in your journal.

1. Pay attention to the world around you, and notice sights, sounds, colors, scents, patterns, textures, etc.
2. Question unquestioned answers.
3. Grab some blank paper, and doodle. Make up stories about your doodling.
4. Travel off beaten paths, and record new experiences.
5. Welcome analogies and metaphors into your life. (For example, my car is like... because; this clock is like ... because; how is this difficult customer like a pencil?; etc.)
6. Tear pictures and words out of magazines, and paste them into a collage that reflects your goals and dreams.

7. Go outside and look up at the clouds. See how many different pictures you can see.

8. Let out your wonderfully imaginative child within by playing games, going to the playground, spending time with children playing imaginary games.

9. Develop an unfailing bias for creative loafing.

10. Take 365 'guilt-free' vacations each year. (This means doing something every single day that is fun, different, and exciting. It can be 10 minutes, or the entire day! But every day, build in a mini-vacation!)

11. Schedule a 20-minute meditation time, and sit quietly. You can listen to soft music, light a candle, or use a guided imagery CD. Just allow yourself to visualize whatever comes to mind.

12. Begin capturing your dreams, and reflecting on the messages they bring you.

13. Improve your storytelling ability.

Imagination — Activity Two:

As you think about the specific area you want to work on throughout this course, create a vivid image of yourself successfully achieving your goals. What will it look like? How does it feel? What are you doing, saying, thinking? Who are you with? Make your visualization as specific, broad-reaching, and impactful as you possibly can. Once you have a vivid description, record yourself sharing it. Then, listen to this recording at least twice a day, until you can bring the images to your consciousness effortlessly.

Example: Healthy Eating

My goal: entertaining friends while still eating in a healthy way.

My visualization: I am filled with such amazing energy, as I sit around my kitchen table with a group of my friends, serving them a magnificent meal I have prepared that is healthy and delicious. The aroma of the rich, fresh vegetables fill the air, and I feel so relaxed because I have time to be with my friends. It was so easy to prepare this incredible meal! Everyone is joyful, and people are complimenting me on how wonderful I look, and how great the food tastes. (You get the idea!!)

Imagination Affirmation:

I claim Imagination now. I visualize and imagine how to be the best person and the best Christ I can be.

Understanding

Ability to know, perceive, comprehend, and spiritually "see."

Color: Gold

Apostle: Thomas

Location: Front Forebrain

*I claim Understanding now.
I spiritually know and comprehend
that I am Christ.*

There are two ways of getting understanding. One is by following the guidance of Spirit that dwells within, and the other is to go blindly ahead and learn by hard experience. ... Spiritual understanding is the ability of the mind to apprehend and realize the laws of thought and the relation of ideas one to another.

~ Charles Fillmore
Revealing Word, p. 202

Understanding

Overview

- Apostle: Thomas
- Location: Front Forebrain
- Color: Gold
- Understanding works with Wisdom and Love

UNDERSTANDING is the ability to know, perceive, comprehend, and spiritually "see."

From ego/personality: The ability to know and comprehend based on our senses, thoughts, feelings, and beliefs. We use UNDERSTANDING to know the facts and figures, whether we're talking about a bridge or an atomic bomb.

- *Underdeveloped Understanding* results in a person who has difficulty comprehending and knowing easily, resulting in a diminished ability to perceive beyond the literal.

- *Overdeveloped Understanding* results in a person who comes across as a know-it-all and perceives things that are not there … literally or figuratively.

From elevated consciousness: The ability to know and comprehend based on Ideas, Truths, Principles and Laws that are Divine in nature. We use UNDERSTANDING to be the best person and/or Christ we can be.

$\mathcal{T}$he internet has become a really wonderful tool for learning about something new. The world is at our finger tips. Type in a few words, a click of the mouse, and we sometimes have more information than we ever needed or perhaps wanted to know. During this entire process, we are using our ability to know. First, we have to know and comprehend how to use the computer. We must know what the words mean. We must know what we are looking up. All of these, and more, utilize the Ability of Understanding. Sometimes we know a few pieces of information, and then, as we add more and put the pieces together, they suddenly come together in a new way, just like a big jigsaw puzzle! This is the Ability of Understanding.

The Power/Ability of Understanding is our ability to know, perceive, comprehend and "spiritually see." In today's slang, we would say that Understanding means "I get it!" There are two types of Understanding:

- Intellectual understanding, which is based on the relative realm;

- Spiritual Understanding, which is based on the Oneness or Absolute Realm.

Intellectual understanding is gained mostly through experience and the "school of hard knocks." It is subject to temptation and often used for selfish ends. By combining reasoning with intellectual understanding, we are able to arrive at valid, practical conclusions.

Spiritual Understanding is gained by investing time in the Silence. It results from the quickening of our Spiritual Nature, our Christ Nature. This type of knowledge sometimes includes, and always transcends intellectual understanding. This knowing comes swiftly and arises outside of the reasoning process. It comes as an internal knowing, or perhaps as a still small voice that may seem more like the reflection or echo of something we have heard and/or forgotten.

You may be wondering how this Ability is different from the Ability of Judgment which we studied in an earlier chapter. After all, they both involve knowledge and comprehension. The difference is that the Ability of Understanding focuses on what we know and our ability to put that information into the proper context. However, knowledge, no matter how well understood, is fairly useless unless it can be applied to our daily life and activities. That's when the Ability of Judgment/Wisdom comes in. The Ability of Judgment/Wisdom is more about knowing how to actually use the information in practical and productive ways. Wisdom is knowledge with the ability to use it so that it has bearing on our personal life and activities.

Knowledge gained using the Ability of Understanding is more stable when it is based on Divine Ideas, Principles, and Laws. Spiritual Understanding is the ability to comprehend the Laws of Thought as well as the relation of Divine Ideas to each other. This type of knowledge is unchanging, because it is not based on the ever changing relative realm but on the immutable Laws of Spirit. Spiritual Judgment/Wisdom is the ability to apply those Laws of Thought, recognizing the relation of one Divine Idea to another. It is also the ability to use and apply the knowledge that arises from that internal knowing that is outside and independent of intellectual reasoning.

Now let's look at the use of the Ability of Understanding at the four levels of consciousness we have been exploring:

1. **Unconscious Understanding:** based on a cause in subconscious mind which consists of beliefs that are not in our moment to moment awareness. This would be when a person subconsciously believes s/he is not worthy, and so, no matter what s/he does, s/he approaches it with the unconscious knowing that s/he does not deserve anything.

2. **Conscious Understanding from our senses:** based on something in physicality we are gleaning through our sight, sound, scent, touch, and/or taste. For example, after experiencing the impact of going out into the cold without the proper clothing, a person knows what to wear the next time.

3. **Conscious Understanding from our human personality:** based on thoughts, feelings, attitudes, and/or beliefs held in human consciousness. A person believes s/he can become a doctor and then

goes about doing research in order to know what needs to be done to become a qualified, Board-approved physician.

4. **Conscious Understanding from our True Identity, or Higher Self:** based upon Divine Ideas, Laws, and Principles. This is when we begin to perceive and comprehend that there is more to us than a physical body and an ego, and we understand what it takes to be the best person or Christ we can be.

Understanding: Putting It Into Practice

Understanding — Activity One:

This one should be fun! Grab a piece of colored paper, and cut it into several big pieces, as if you were creating a jigsaw puzzle. Now, imagine that each piece represents some aspect of your job. When these pieces are put together, they will depict all the major components that make up the work you do. Take some time and write an aspect of your job on each piece of the puzzle you have created.

Now, imagine you are coaching someone who is interested in your job. How could you use this puzzle as a way to help that person understand what s/he would need to know or comprehend in order to have a grasp of what your work involves?

What did this activity tell you about the Power/Ability of Understanding? What role does Understanding play in successfully achieving your goals?

Understanding — Activity Two:

As you think about the specific area you want to work on throughout this course, brainstorm the specific things you need to know and understand to be successful. Include items from both the sense level and the more elevated Spiritual level.

You might start by writing the sentence: In order to be successful in the area I am working on throughout this course, I need to know:

Now, complete that sentence ten different ways!

Example: Healthy Eating

In order to eat more healthily, I need to know what the recommended daily food requirements are; which foods meet these requirements; what amounts are appropriate each day; how to combine these foods into manageable, edible meals ...

From a Spiritual level, I need to know how to develop my intuitive sense of knowing what to eat and when.

Understanding Affirmation:

I claim Understanding now. I spiritually know and comprehend that I am the best person and Christ I can be.

*Understanding is a fountain of life
to those who have it.*

~ Proverbs 16:22

Will

Ability to choose, decide, command, direct, and determine.

Color: Silver

Apostle: Matthew

Location: Front Forebrain

I claim Will now. I use Will to choose to be the best Christ I can be.

Will

Overview

- Apostle: Matthew
- Location: Front Forebrain
- Color: Silver
- Works with Understanding, Wisdom and Love.

WILL is the ability to choose, decide, command, direct, and determine.

From ego/personality: The ability to choose, decide, command, lead, and determine based on the senses, thoughts, feelings, and beliefs. We use WILL to make life-enhancing choices ... or not.

- *Underdeveloped Will* results in a person that is indecisive, is wishy-washy and cannot make a decision.

- *Overdeveloped Will* results in willful people that must have their own way all the time. They exhibit a "my way or the highway" attitude. They are obstinate as well as have a "don't confuse me with the facts" attitude. Once a decision is made they are loathed to change it. They are also bossy and tell everyone what to do.

From elevated consciousness: The ability to choose, decide, command, lead, and determine based on Ideas, Truths, Principles and Laws that are Divine in nature. We use WILL to choose and direct all thoughts and actions to be the best person and/or Christ we can be.

*T*hink about the incredible number of choices you make every single day. From the moment you open your eyes in the morning (or whenever it is you choose to arise), you choose whether to get out of bed or hit the snooze button and snuggle under the covers for a few more minutes of rest; you choose what to wear; what to have for breakfast; what to read or listen to as you grab that breakfast you chose; and what your schedule will look like for the day. By the time you actually get your day started, you have already made hundreds of tiny choices, mostly without any conscious thought at all! This is fine, because we could drive ourselves batty if we had to pay a lot of attention to every single choice we make. However, the problem comes when we make important choices the same way we decide what to eat for breakfast: by default rather than intention. Imagine how powerful your life could be if you called on your most elevated level of consciousness to make the important choices in your life. That is what the Ability of Will is all about!

Making choices involves the Abilities we have already explored and those that are yet to come; all of the Abilities are in play in our choice-making. However, the Ability of Will is the one we use to actually make the choice. It is often called the executive power of mind. In addition to the ability to choose and decide, it is also the ability to command and direct. It actually moves all the other Abilities into action. Think about it. We choose:

- What we believe. (Faith)
- When, where and for what we stay the course. (Strength)
- What we judge and when we apply what we know. (Judgment)
- What we desire, need, require and for whom we have the highest regard. (Love)
- What we master or have dominion over. (Power/Dominion)
- What we visualize. (Imagination)
- What we know. (Understanding)
- When and what we organize, sequence or adjust. (Order)
- What we are passionate about. (Zeal)
- What we deny or get rid of. (Elimination)
- What we vitalize or enliven. (Life)

We realize you may not be familiar with some of the Abilities listed above ... it is a sneak peak into our future chapters! Hopefully, it will whet your appetite as we continue exploring each Ability individually, and it will also help you see how all the Abilities work together, much like the cast of a play. In fact, if we used the analogy of a play, then the Ability of Will would be the Director.

Let's go back to an example we used earlier to see if we can make this more practical. In a broad and general way, life boils down to a series of judgments and choices:

1. First you make a judgment about whether you want something in your life. The underlying decision is basically reduced to: is it good for me or bad for me? Do I want it or not? The Ability of Judgment discerns one thing from another. Will is the ability we use to actually make the choice for one or the other.

2. After you decide you want something (it is good), another judgment is made: who is going to get it or make sure it happens. You could get it yourself, work with someone else to get it, or convince someone else to get it for you. The Ability of Judgment evaluates one from the other. The actual choice of who gets it would use the Ability of Will.

3. In the case where you decide you do not want it in your life (it is bad or at least not good), another judgment is made concerning who is going to remove it from your life. You could remove it yourself, work with someone else to remove it, or convince someone else to remove it for you. The Ability of Judgment is involved in discerning one choice from the other. The Ability of Will actually makes the choice.

This matter of choice is a very interesting one. Hopefully, most of us learn by experience over time how to make the wisest choices. However, have you ever judged what would be best in a situation, and actually made another choice anyway? Many of us can remember when we were teenagers and knew we should not do something, yet did it anyway. Perhaps you were grounded and decided to sneak out the window to meet with your friends. Maybe even today you know not to speed on a certain street because there is frequently a speed trap there .... yet you do it anyway. Many drink and drive. And we are appalled that there needs to be a law prohibiting texting and driving! Who would have thought anyone would choose to do that?

All these examples illustrate the Ability of Will in action. Even though we may know the right thing to do, we can still use our Ability of Will, the ability to choose, to make another choice! We'd say this is yet another definition of insanity: knowing the best choice and making a different one!

At this point, we ask your indulgence while we take a bit of a side trip to clear up a common misunderstanding. In our experience teaching the Ability of Will, we have noticed a tendency on the part of some of our students to confuse the Power/Ability of Will with what they call God's Will (or God-Will). We hear people ask, "What is God's Will for my life?" This question comes from a belief that God has a specific will for them, a kind of Divine Plan or predetermination, where God has already made all the choices for their lives. From this perspective, their Power/Ability of Will would be limited and restricted to their capacity to make choices about whether or not to follow the Divine Plan labeled as God's Will.

We believe this whole idea stems from the religious practices in which people were raised. This kind of interpretation of God's Will implies a separation – a sense of an anthropomorphic God out there, micromanaging our lives. In actuality, the Will of God is non-specific for any of our lives and circumstances. The Divine Plan is for each of us to make the very best choices to express the maximum amount of Goodness, Godness, and Christ consciousness we can at our present level of awareness ... And we do this by using our Power/Ability of Will at its highest level.

Thanks for indulging us! Now, let's get back to our discussion of the Power/Ability of Will. As with all the Powers/Abilities, we can use Will from different levels of consciousness. Choices based on our sense consciousness, or ego/personality, can range from very good and appropriate to the "what was I thinking" level of dismay! Since our senses tend to be rather selective in terms of accepting and sorting incoming information, what they seem to report should always be suspect. Because our shifting moods and focus tend to affect how we interpret incoming information, our human use of the Ability of Will should always be questioned.

On the other hand, the use of the Ability of Will informed from a higher spiritual awareness is more certain. Our goal is to claim for ourselves the Truth of What (not who) we are, Christ. We have the capacity to so identify ourselves with Divine Mind that we can align ourselves in every thought and deed from the awareness of Divine Ideas, Laws, and Principles.

One area for vigilance is a tendency to subjugate ourselves to the will of another. Sure, there are always exceptions, like minors and mentally incapacitated adults. And of course, there are many times when we use Will to choose to go along with someone else's idea, or cooperate for the good of the whole. But it should always be a conscious choice; by and large, we don't want to allow others to determine our path and direction. And of course, the converse is also true: we do not want to inflict our will upon another.

We should also be aware of states of consciousness leading to the more negative side or down side of the Ability of Will. We certainly want to avoid becoming willful or stubborn. When we are willful, we force our decisions and choices upon another. When we are stubborn, we tend to ignore the facts and not change our minds (make another choice) for a variety of reasons, ranging from not wanting to be wrong (wanting to be right) to simply wanting our own way regardless of the consequences.

Now let's look at the use of the Ability of Will at the four levels of consciousness we have been exploring:

1. **Unconscious Will:** based on a cause in our subconscious mind which consists of beliefs that are not in our moment to moment awareness. Choices are made from unconscious/subconscious beliefs, by default rather than a conscious choice. For example, if a person has a subconscious belief that s/he is unworthy, then choices will be unwittingly made that reinforce this belief.

2. **Conscious Will from our senses:** based on something in physicality we are gleaning through our sight, sound, scent, touch, and or taste. A person might decide to turn right instead of left because there is heavy traffic to left, and s/he knows of another way to get home by turning left.

3. **Conscious Will from our human personality:** based on thoughts, feelings, attitudes and/or beliefs held in human consciousness. A person believes that s/he can become a doctor. After gathering the information and reviewing the requirements, s/he makes the choice to move ahead with that career option.

4. **Conscious Will from our True Identity, or Higher Self:** based on Divine Ideas, Laws, and Principles. We make choices and decisions that reinforce and confirm our belief in our True, Christ Nature.

Will:
Putting It Into Practice

Will — Activity One:

For one day, make decisions quickly and act on them. For example, when you are getting dressed, walk into your closet and choose the first thing you see. What movie to see? Pick one right off the top of your head; when you are in a restaurant, glance at the menu and choose something immediately. You get the idea!

At the end of the day, reflect on your experience:

• What role did Will play?

• What impact did some of the other Abilities we've discussed have (especially Judgment and Understanding)?

• How accurate were your snap decisions?

• How did it feel to make decisions so quickly?

- What does this tell you about your Ability of Will and how effectively you use it?

Will — Activity Two:

As you think about the specific area you want to work on throughout this course, make a list of some of the important choices you have made up to this week, and evaluate their effectiveness.
- What choices would you like to change? Can you? How?
- What choices do you need to make at this point, to move you forward in being successful with your goal?

Example: Healthy Eating

Key Choices up to this point:

I chose to set boundaries with my mom about how she could help support me on this journey toward healthy eating. (Effectiveness: Excellent! Mom was more supportive than I could have hoped for – and she has come up with some healthy variations of some of my old favorites!)

Choice I'd like to change:

I chose to go with my friend to Dairy Queen, and I caved! I ordered a large chocolate chip cookie dough Blizzard ... and ate the whole thing! (I can't change it since I've already eaten the whole thing ... but I can learn that this is a potential temptation for me. I want to prepare a way to handle future invitations such as this more effectively.)

Will Affirmation:

I claim Will now. I use Will to choose to be the best person and the best Christ I can be.

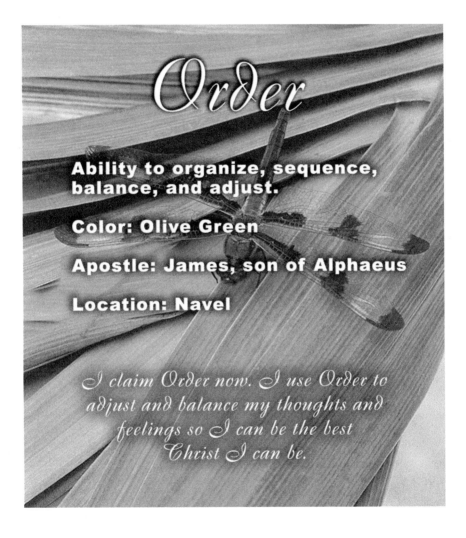

Order

Ability to organize, sequence, balance, and adjust.

Color: Olive Green

Apostle: James, son of Alphaeus

Location: Navel

I claim Order now. I use Order to adjust and balance my thoughts and feelings so I can be the best Christ I can be.

Order

Overview

- Apostle: James son of Alphaeus
- Location: Navel
- Color: Olive Green
- Works with Love to create harmony

ORDER is the ability to organize, sequence, balance, and adjust.

From ego/personality: The ability to organize, sequence, balance, and adjust, based on our senses, thoughts, feelings and beliefs. We use ORDER to organize the garage or create a logical sequence to accomplish something ~ or, we can use it to be obsessive compulsive.

- *Underdeveloped Order* results in someone who cannot organize, balance, or make adjustments easily. You might call a person with underdeveloped Order disorganized, disorderly, or even (to the extreme) slovenly. They find it very difficult to adjust to change.

- *Overdeveloped Order* results in someone who is overly fastidious about their immediate environment, must make sure everything is just so, and may be obsessive compulsive, as well as hyper-detailed about nearly everything. This person obsesses over every picture being perfectly level and in precisely the right position.

From elevated consciousness: The ability to organize, sequence, balance, and adjust based on Ideas, Truths, Principles, and Laws that are Divine in nature. We use ORDER to adjust and organize our thoughts, feelings, and actions to be the best person and/or Christ we can be.

$\mathcal{T}$hink about the messiest place in your home. We know, this is not the most enjoyable thing you could be thinking about! But bear with us for just a moment. It might be the garage, the office, a bedroom, a closet, or maybe just that catch-all drawer in the kitchen. How many times have you had thoughts about cleaning up, and getting that particular area in order? You were using your Ability of Imagination linked with the Ability of Order ... and when you actually start the clean-up process, the Ability of Order kicks in even more, since you use it to adjust what you imagined as you go along. As you invest your time and energy creating a special place for each thing, you can literally feel a sense of organization and balance flow through your very being!

Order, like so many of the other Abilities, is often misunderstood. People sometimes get confused and use the phrase Divine Order, meaning Divine Will, Divine Predetermination, or Divine Proclamation. As stated in the book, *Get Over It,* by Paul Hasselbeck and Bil Holton, "It [Divine Order] is often used in the traditional sense [meaning] there is a God outside of us ordering everything that happens in the universe, including our daily lives. The idea is that there is a set order for our lives and that all of our activities are governed by it." This misunderstanding of Divine Order leaves one feeling resigned rather than empowered.

Understood in a different and more empowering way, Divine Order is the orderly sequence by which everything comes into existence: Mind-Idea-Expression. Everyone ... and we do mean everyone ... uses this sequence; we cannot not use it! First there is an idea or thought in mind; we experience it; and then we go about bringing the thought or idea into physical existence—or not. In the case of cleaning out that messy area we envisioned to kick off this chapter, you probably thought about cleaning it a lot prior to actually bringing the act into physical existence!

There are many things we have thought about doing and have never done. We may have experienced it to some extent in our minds, but have not experienced it in the physical realm. The Ability of Order is the ability to organize, and shows up in our lives in the way we organize our living space, work, files, and lives. We use it to sequence a series of activities to reach a goal, or to schedule the classes we need to take to complete a degree, or even to arrange the ingredients we put into a recipe. We use it to make plans as well as to adjust those plans according to what we encounter along the way. For example, you are driving to a friend's house and find your usual way obstructed by emergency road work. In that moment you will use the Ability of Order to adjust to this new situation and re-sequence the way you get to your destination. (Of course, all of this is done more wisely if the Abilities of Judgment and Understanding are engaged—but don't let that confuse you!)

When the Ability of Order is underdeveloped, you will not be able to create much balance in your life, nor will you find it easy to adjust to changes. Further, there will be the inhibited ability to sequence events and activities. As a result, you will feel disorganized, and find yourself backtracking or re-doing things in order to finish a project. Your home and work environments may well be messy and disorganized, even though you probably claim that you know where to find everything you need!

When the Ability of Order is overdeveloped, you tend to be very fastidious and obsessive about everything having a place and being in it ... to perfection. There will be a compulsiveness about things being done in a certain way and order. Think about a person who sits down to dinner in a restaurant, and re-organizes the place setting while defining their space. They adjust the location of the water glass, and even where the salt and pepper shakers are at the center of the table. If you happen to be dining with this person and move the salt and pepper shakers, they will invariably move them back to where they had originally positioned them.

It is also useful to review how the Ability of Order is used at various levels of consciousness:

1. **Unconscious Order:** based on a cause in our subconscious mind which consists of beliefs that are not in our moment to moment awareness. In this case, you would organize, sequence, and adjust your life to conform to a belief you are not even aware of. For example a person who has a subconscious belief in unworthiness might win the lottery, and then organize, sequence, and adjust their actions so the money is lost in a short period of time. Then they would say, "I don't know why this happened to me!"

2. **Conscious Order from our senses:** based on something in physicality we are gleaning through our sight, sound, scent, touch, or taste. This is that person who must have the picture just so, the place setting just right, or the garage in perfect order.

3. **Conscious Order from our human personality:** based on thoughts, feelings, attitudes and/or beliefs held in human consciousness. In the case of becoming a doctor, the person will organize, sequence, and adjust life so s/he obtains the goal. The person will take all the pre-med courses in the right order, and then take the pre-med exam (Med-Cat) the next time the course is given after s/he is prepared and ready.

4. **Conscious Order from our True Identity, or Higher Self:** based on the Divine Ideas, Laws, and Principles. Here, we use Order to organize, balance, sequence, and make adjustments so we can be the Christ that we already are. We might notice that we are showing up in very egotistic and unproductive ways, and then re-adjust our ways of being to be the best Christ we can be.

Order:
Putting It Into Practice

Order — Activity One:

Go back to that area of messiness you thought of at the beginning of this chapter. If you did not choose a specific area yet, this is the moment. Choose an area in your living environment that is out of order, cluttered, untidy, and somewhat chaotic.

Schedule a block of time, and put it in order. Create a space that is balanced, orderly, neat, and efficient for what you need.

Once you are done, grab your journal and jot down answers to the following questions:

- What inner feelings did you experience as you ordered this area of your life?

- What other Abilities did you see interacting with Order, to help you achieve this goal?

Order — Activity Two

As you think about the specific area you want to work on throughout this course, identify the areas involving sequencing, adjusting, ordering, and balancing that are necessary to achieve your goal successfully. Create a schedule (that would be using Order) to address the areas that need some work.

Example: Healthy Eating

I need to create an eating plan for the week, so I can plan my grocery shopping, my cooking, and the foods I will be eating. I also need to coordinate my work schedule in with my eating plan, to plan for those meetings that are conducted in restaurants.

Order Affirmation:

I claim Order now. I use Order to adjust and balance my thoughts and feelings so I can be the best person and the best Christ I can be.

The universal order and the personal order are nothing but different expressions and manifestations of a common underlying principle.

~ Marcus Aurelius

Zeal

Ability to be enthusiastic and passionate, as well as to inspire and motivate oneself.

Color: Orange

Apostle: Simon the Canaanite

Location: Medulla Oblongata (Brain Stem, Back of the Neck)

I claim Zeal now. I use Zeal to be passionate and enthusiastic about being the best Christ I can be.

Zeal/Enthusiasm

Overview

- Apostle: Simon the Canaanite
- Location: Medulla Oblongata, Brain Stem, back of the neck
- Color: Orange

Zeal is the ability to be enthusiastic and passionate, as well as to inspire and motivate oneself.

From ego/personality: The ability to be enthusiastic, passionate, inspirational, and motivational based on our senses, thoughts, feelings, and beliefs.

- *Underdeveloped Zeal* results in a person who is listless and has little zest for life. The person would be personally unmotivated, and unable to inspire others. Starting things would be extremely difficult, let alone seeing things through to completion.

- *Overdeveloped Zeal* results in a person who is zealous, impulsive, ruthless, compulsive, and overly ambitious. This individual often comes across way too strong, and ends up appearing to be insincere and phony.

From elevated consciousness: The ability to be enthusiastic, passionate, inspirational, and motivational based on Ideas, Truths, Principles, and Laws that are Divine in Nature. We use Zeal to enthusiastically be the best person and/or Christ we can be.

$\mathcal{H}$ave you ever had a friend or relative get involved in some multilevel marketing opportunity? Sometime people are simply excited and enthusiastic about the products because they have used them and liked them, and they want you to know about it. Others are more like religious zealots, pressuring you and pushing their products to the point of being obnoxious. If you are like us, we tend to want to avoid these encounters. These examples represent how the Ability of Zeal can be used in supportive, positive ways or adverse, negative ways, especially when informed from sense consciousness/personality.

Let's take another example, straight from the Bible. Many people are aware of the Apostle Paul. Prior to his conversion on the road to Damascus (Acts 9), he was known as Saul of Tarsus. He was zealous about stomping out the newly emerging sect that developed around Jesus and his teachings. Simon turned in any followers of this new sect to the Jewish authorities ... and he was proud of his work! If you were a member of this sect, your perception of the way he went about this would be a good example of the negative use of the Ability of Zeal. However, if you were a member of the ruling Jewish authorities, you would perceive this as a good thing. After his conversion, Saul became known as Paul and continued to be very zealous. However, now he utilized his Ability of Zeal to promote and spread the growing sect that came to be known as Christianity. In fact, many of the books of the Christian Scriptures are letters written by Paul to various churches he helped found. Many would agree that the Christian sect would have probably died out if not for Paul's zealousness and passion. Some would agree that Paul was using his Ability of Zeal in a productive and positive way.

There are a multitude of modern day examples of the use of Ability of Zeal in the context of religion. Certainly, suicide bombers and those who go to any lengths to promote and promulgate their religious views are examples. Many would view this as an adverse use of Zeal. On the other hand, someone like Mother Teresa is usually viewed as a good example of a supportive and uplifting use of the Ability of Zeal. Her work in the streets of Calcutta demonstrates the use of Zeal from the moment she chose to see the face of Jesus in that first person she lifted in her arms. It blossomed into a lifelong passion, again using the Ability of Zeal.

Over our lifetimes most of us have experienced a passion for something, whether it is our favorite TV show or a popular sports team. Some people collect stamps, coins, or vintage pottery from the last century. Others have a passion for rock climbing, ballroom dancing, or model railroading. Regardless of the object of our passion, we are using the Ability of Zeal.

If you're like us, you can feel a bit like a detective when entering somebody else's home. A lot can be learned about another person's passions by simply observing their surroundings. This is particularly interesting going to estate sales. One witnesses the evidence of a well-lived life. In one estate sale there might be a multitude of owl figurines, in another elephants, in another a completely decked out workshop. Wherever you find a human being, you will likely find some passion.

This is also true when you go to someone's office. In fact, good sales people pay particular attention to the pictures, book titles, and memorabilia the buyer has in the office. They then use the information gleaned to start conversations, and build a sense of trust.

Passions can last anywhere from a short period of time to a lifetime. Some people dive into one activity after another, while other people stick to one thing for a lifetime. Whatever the passion, the Ability of Zeal is behind it. In addition, anytime we start something, Zeal is the Ability we activate whether we know it or not.

The Ability of Zeal is our ability to be enthusiastic, zealous, and passionate. It is also our ability to inspire, start, or motivate ourselves. Zeal is like the first stage of a two-stage rocket: the burst of energy lifting the rocket off the launch pad. After getting the rocket going, the fuel is spent and the second stage must take over. Zeal is like this! Our zeal or enthusiasm for something can burn out quickly, leaving things undone.

This is where the second stage comes into play. For the rocket, the second stage keeps it going until it reaches its goal, escape velocity, and orbits around the earth. With Zeal, we combine a few other Abilities to ensure this second phase kicks in. We use the Ability of Life (which we discuss in more detail later), that enlivens and energizes whatever we are doing. In addition, when Zeal starts to wane, we must engage the Ability of Strength to stay the course and keep on going. We could say that Strength is the determination to see something through to the goal after we used Zeal to get us started. We may also engage Dominion to control any thoughts or feelings about quitting.

Here's a great example! Think about what we call "the spiritual book of the month" when a new book is released, surrounded by lots of hype and marketing. You read it and get very excited about it. In fact, you may even get zealous about it, telling all your friends and writing testimonials on Amazon. Then, when the next book comes along, the teachings of the previous book are all but forgotten when you now zealously embrace the next book. In this case, you certainly had the enthusiasm/zeal for the new book and its teachings, but fell short of continuing to energize these teachings because you are now giving your intention and attention to the next offering.

Someone with underdeveloped Zeal has little zest for life, can be listless, and has difficulty getting started with anything. This person probably has a slew of unfinished projects around the house, or a long to-do list of things which have not even been started. Not only does this person lack self-motivation; inspiring others is difficult or seemingly impossible.

We have already taken a look at overdeveloped zeal in the case of the Apostle Paul and the multilevel marketer. Overdeveloped Zeal shows up as excessive passion for something. In fact, these people can be seen as a bit obsessive-compulsive. However, even this can be used in productive ways. The Ringling Brothers Circus museum, located in Sarasota, Florida, is home to the world's largest miniature circus, captured down to the minutest detail. The Howard Bros. Circus Model is a 3/4-inch scale model depicting Ringling Bros. and Barnum & Bailey Circus when it was at its largest (circa 1919-1938). Occupying 3,800 square feet, it contains eight main tents, 152 wagons, 1,300 circus performers and workers, more than 800 animals, and a 57-car train. Howard Tibbals, the creator of this masterpiece, invested an incredible number of hours over a 50-year period to create this model. He must have had a mighty passion to complete such a marvelous project. One could perceive this as either a magnificent passion or an obsession. Whatever the view, it still resulted in a wonderful gift for all to see.

Let's explore how the Ability of Zeal is used at various levels of consciousness:

1. **Unconscious Zeal:** based on a cause in our subconscious mind which consists of beliefs that are not in our moment to moment awareness. A person with unconscious Zeal would be enthusiastic about doing something, and clueless about the reason. For example, a person may get excited and totally enthusiastic about a piece of music, and be totally unaware that the response is triggered by a belief or memory from the past. Experiences like this happen quite often because of experiences held in the subconscious mind from childhood. Realtors suggest burning scented candles or baking cookies prior to a person viewing a home for sale because these aromas can trigger subconscious memories and beliefs from childhood that ignite enthusiasm to buy the home.

2. **Conscious Zeal from our senses:** based on something in physicality we are gleaning through our sight, sound, scent, touch and or taste. For example, a child enters the shopping mall and spies a beautiful carrousel. She loves to ride the carrousel and so enthusiastically runs (motivates herself) toward the carrousel.

3. **Conscious Zeal from our human personality:** based on thoughts, feelings, attitudes and/or beliefs held in human consciousness. A young man knows and believes that exercise is good for his body, and believes eating all the right foods is the very best for his health. As a result, he is zealous about getting his exercise and eating right, even in the face of a multitude of temptations.

4. **Conscious Zeal from our True Identity, or Higher Self:** based on Divine Ideas, Laws, and Principles. Once you get a glimpse and experience of your Spiritual Nature, you experience a passion and zeal about learning more and about being the best Christ you can be. You passionately start to research and discover more, so you can have more of these experiences.

Zeal:
Putting It Into Practice

Zeal — Activity One:

This is a "High Five" Activity!

Part 1: Grab your journal and respond quickly to the following questions:

- What are five things I really enjoy doing?
- What are my five strongest skills and/or gifts?
- Who are five people I find inspiring and motivational?
- What are five of my favorite books, movies, TV shows, and/or sporting events?
- What are five of my favorite quotes?

Part 2: Reflect on your responses above, using the following thought provokers to help you:

- What do the answers to the questions above tell me about myself, in terms of what inspires and motivate me?
- What are common themes or patterns, in terms of how I experience the Ability of Zeal in my life?
- How does Zeal manifest as I express it?
- How can I begin to consciously call on the Ability of Zeal when I may not be feeling it?
- How are the other Abilities interacting with Zeal, as I am involved in my favorite activities identified above?

Zeal — Activity Two

As you think about the specific area you want to work on throughout this course, identify ways you can claim and activate the Ability of Zeal to help you be successful. Here's an interesting side note: When he was 94, Charles Fillmore wrote this statement: "I fairly sizzle with zeal and enthusiasm, and spring forth with a mighty faith to do the things that ought to done by me!" What affirmations could you write to spur you to action? Come up with a few, and then say them often, using lots of enthusiasm and excitement. We are serious here! You might even over-act it! Say the affirmations as if you were a college football coach at half time, spurring the team on to victory! Get excited, and use your Zeal to bring energy to your statements. Notice the difference it makes in your ability to be successful!

Example: Healthy Eating

I can claim Zeal by having a friend who supports my goal go with me to restaurants. Together, we can play a game zealously and passionately, finding the healthiest combination of foods on the menu. We can create an award for ourselves whenever we successfully consume a healthy meal in a restaurant!

Affirmations I can use:

- I am radiantly healthy, and feel great because I eat food that is good for my body.
- I love and accept my body completely! I am good to my body and my body is good to me!
- Nothing tastes as great as healthy feels!

Zeal Affirmation:

I claim Zeal now. I use Zeal to be passionate and enthusiastic about being the best person and the best Christ I can be.

Do not let your zeal run away with your judgment. When zeal and judgment work together, great things can be accomplished!

~ Charles Fillmore
Revealing Word, p. 216

Elimination

Ability to release, remove, denounce, deny, say no, and let go.

Color: Russet

Apostle: Thaddeus

Location: Lower Abdominal Region

I claim Elimination now. I deny and eliminate anything that I have empowered to hinder my being the best Christ I can be.

Elimination/Release

Overview

- Apostle: Thaddeus
- Location: Lower Abdominal Region
- Color: Russet

ELIMINATION/RELEASE is the ability to release, remove, denounce, deny, say no, and let go.

From ego/personality: The ability to release, remove, denounce, deny, say no, and let go based on our senses, thoughts, feelings, and beliefs. Elimination releases and lets go of things that are not working or are no longer useful in our lives. We use ELIMINATION to release a habit like smoking or biting our nails, or, ironically, we may use Elimination to release and let go of things that are working, like an exercise program or meditation practice.

- *Underdeveloped Elimination* results in the classic pack rat, people who have difficulty getting rid of anything. They have a hard time ending relationships, jobs, or other situations … even bad or abusive friendships or relationships.
- *Overdeveloped Elimination* results in person who is rash about what is eliminated or renounced. There are pre-mature endings of relationships and jobs. This person could be wasteful, purging all the time, and might throw the baby out with the bathwater.

From elevated consciousness: The ability to release, remove, denounce, deny, and let go based on Ideas, Truths, Principles, and Laws that are Divine in nature. We use ELIMINATION to let go of anything that interferes with these Ideas or erroneously uses Divine Laws and Principles. We use ELIMINATION to let go of old beliefs/embedded theology, and aspects of our ego/personality that hinder being the best person and/or Christ we can be.

*H*ave you ever experienced an excessively cluttered home? We don't want to get personal here, so let's talk about places we've seen — and you can call up your own experiences. We saw a show on TV featuring a woman who had held on to so much stuff there was only a narrow path left for walking through every room of her house! We've seen other homes where every single flat surface is covered. Each square inch is piled with papers, knick-knacks, and other stuff.

On the other hand, we've visited in homes that are very minimalist, where the decor is sparse with no excess—the closets, garage, and basement appear barren. All these examples represent environments that are evidence of the Ability of Elimination.

In order to say yes, we must also be able to say no. Please read that sentence again, and allow it to internalize! (Go ahead, we'll wait!) Using the Ability of Elimination allows us to say no to the things that no longer serve us, including thoughts, beliefs, people, and stuff! We use the Ability of Elimination to say no, whether it is to something in consciousness or in the outer, physical realm. We must be able to renounce, eliminate, and say no in order to change our minds and consciousness, as well as to be able to eliminate useless stuff from our lives. Of course, the Ability of Judgment must be engaged, to evaluate whether it is appropriate to say yes or no.

The Ability of Elimination is the Ability behind denials. It is the ability we use to disempower thoughts, feelings, and beliefs. If we truly want to grow in the awareness of our Spiritual Nature, we must be able to deny, disempower, and let go of any thoughts, feelings, and beliefs that hinder or hold us back, or keep us tied to our personalities/ego. We cannot effectively claim our True Nature if at the same time we believe we are simply personalities inhabiting physical bodies.

All of us carry conscious or subconscious beliefs that we chose at sometime in our lives as a way to take care of ourselves. At some point, these beliefs are no longer useful. Many people are raised in a belief system consisting of an external God that is a supernatural Being having absolute control and power over them. For some, this belief system serves them well their entire lives, while for others, this belief system loses its appeal. This leads them to search for, and hopefully find a new belief system that works better. However, since the old belief system was held in consciousness for so long, it may still have a hold at barely conscious, if not subconscious levels. By using their Ability of Elimination/Renunciation, these people are able to disempower and eliminate every aspect of the old belief system in order to fully embrace the new.

There are many examples of this Power/Ability at work in the physical world. Our physical bodies are a great example of the Ability of Elimination at work. When we breathe in, we acquire oxygen and we must let go of carbon dioxide in order to survive. We take in food and give off waste. If we did not release these metabolic waste products, we would surely die. When we exercise, we release excess heat through perspiration and heavy breathing. If we did not do this, we could become overheated and die. We bring groceries into our homes and we release garbage, keeping our homes neat and tidy. Where there is inflow or increase, there also must be outflow and release. The Dead Sea is void of life because there is inflow but no outflow.

Underdeveloped Ability of Elimination is demonstrated by people who are pack rats or hoarders. They collect and hold onto everything … even useless and broken stuff. In fact, you could get a nosebleed climbing over their stacks of newspapers and magazines! Sometimes these folks become emotionally attached to their stuff, and become upset or distressed at the very suggestion of releasing it.

The Underdeveloped Ability of Elimination is also seen in people who simply cannot end things like jobs or relationships, even when they are harmful. These people might be able to sort the wheat from the chaff, the good from the bad—but they simply cannot eliminate any of it. They just keep hanging on, justifying it by assuming that at least they know what to expect.

Many of us have had the experience of being unable to let go of things that are good, when we have welcomed "the better" into our lives. For example, we might have a perfectly good hot water heater, but decide to get a more efficient instantaneous hot water heater. And then, guess what? That good, old hot water heater sits in the garage or basement simply because we could not part with it. If the water heater example is too big a stretch for you, what about this one? How many articles of clothing hang in your closet unused for years, even though you have newer, more up-to-date, better fitting clothes to replace them? (Are we getting too personal now?) As we learn to use our Ability of Elimination effectively, we find it useful to remind ourselves of this affirmation: I let go of my good to make room for my greater good!

Let's look at this from a spiritual point of view. We may clearly believe in God being Divine Mind—not an external supernatural, perhaps male, Being. We may believe in Oneness— One Power and One Presence. And, yet, in some of our actions, like prayer, we are still holding on to the "old God" by addressing God as "He" and as a Being who is separate and apart ... expecting guidance and direction from "out there."

Overdeveloped Elimination results in getting rid of things prematurely. For example, have you ever eliminated some perfectly good possession, then later needed to re-purchase them?

The overdeveloped Ability of Elimination can also manifest as denying valuable ideas and beliefs before really understanding their usefulness. For example, someone could be taking a class and learning some new metaphysical principles, and dismiss them out of hand. Another case involved a man who needed new flooring in his lower level living area and kitchen. A trusted friend suggested simply putting a high grade finish on the concrete. The man quickly said no, without really investigating or considering the idea.

Let's examine how the Ability of Elimination is used at various levels of consciousness:

1. **Unconscious Elimination:** based on a cause in our subconscious mind which consists of beliefs that are not in our moment to moment awareness. If a person has an unconscious or subconscious belief based on something from the past, s/he might unconsciously eliminate things that challenge that belief. A great example would be a woman who clips coupons and saves every penny, won't release any extra funds for things she really needs, and does not

even leave a tip at a restaurant – even though she has plenty of money flowing in her life. She eliminates any signs of prosperity in her life, because of a subconscious fear of lack, arising from her parents who went through the depression.

2. **Conscious Elimination from our senses:** based on something in physicality we are gleaning through our sight, sound, scent, touch, and or taste. We have all probably smelled something spoiling in our refrigerators and proceeded to eliminate its source. Another example is a woman who saw herself doing a presentation on videotape. Based on the way she looked, she decided to institute a diet and exercise program to eliminate her excess weight, and achieve a more desirable body image.

3. **Conscious Elimination from our human personality:** based on thoughts, feelings, attitudes and/or beliefs held in human consciousness. A person might believe that walking under a ladder causes bad luck and so eliminates walking under ladders. A woman married a man she thought was her perfect partner. Over time he became physically and mentally abusive. She believed he would physically harm or even kill her, and used her Ability of Elimination to leave him.

4. **Conscious Elimination from our True Identity, or Higher Self:** based on Divine Ideas, Laws, and Principles. Once aware of how to be the best Christ one can be, a person would then eliminate activities, thoughts, feelings, and beliefs that would inhibit reaching that goal. We can notice situations in which we get angry or fearful and realize that these reactions hinder our being the Christ we can be. So, we first discern the beliefs that fuel the anger or fear, and then use the Ability of Elimination to disempower and remove them from our consciousness.

Elimination: Putting It Into Practice

Elimination — Activity One:

Part 1:

Here is a little experiment to try. In your journal, write the following word:

NO

Say the word out loud. Say it again, louder. Shout it out, with power and gusto! There! You have proved you know how to say no!

Now, write the following word:

KNOW

Say that word. Say it again, louder. Shout it out, with power and gusto!

Did you notice that the two words sound the same? Here's the deal: if you find yourself having trouble saying "No" to things you need to eliminate, just say "Know!" Other people will hear the same thing ... and so will your subconscious mind.

Now let's take it a step further, because there is a very important principle at work here. The key is: *if you KNOW why you want or need to say NO to something, it is a whole lot easier to say it.* In other words, if you have your Christ image clearly in your consciousness, have clarified your goals, and understand your values, you know what will help facilitate those desires, and what is getting in the way. This makes it much easier to say "NO" and release those things which are no longer serving you.

Part 2:

Brainstorm a list of specific things you are willing to let go of, willingly employing your Ability of Elimination, in the following areas:
- Physical (material things, a.k.a. STUFF):
- Mental (attitudes and emotions you are hanging on to):
- Spiritual (outdated beliefs about God; embedded theology).

Elimination — Activity Two:

As you think about the specific area you want to work on throughout this course, identify anything that is no longer serving you in achieving your goal. Write these things down, and conduct a some kind of ceremony, such as burning them in a bowl or fireplace, conducting a symbolic burial, or performing some other ritual to help you release and let these things go!

Example: Healthy Eating

Release and let go of my belief that only chips, crackers, and other high-calorie/high-carb munchies can be tasty snacks.

Release my "big size" clothing that I'm keeping "just in case" I gain back weight.

Elimination Affirmation:

I claim Elimination now. I deny and eliminate anything that I have empowered to hinder my being the best person and the best Christ I can be.

Lay not up for yourselves treasures upon earth, where moth and rust doth corrupt, and where thieves break through and steal: but lay up for yourselves treasures in heaven, where neither moth nor rust doth corrupt, and where thieves do not break through nor steal. For where your treasure is, there will your heart be also.

~ Matthew 6:19-21

Life

Ability to energize, vitalize, enliven, make whole.

Color: Red

Apostle: Judas

Location: The Generative Organs, External Reproductive Organs

I claim Life now. I use Life to energize and enliven my pursuit of being the best Christ I can be.

Life is divine, spiritual, and its source is God, Spirit. The river of life is within [us] in [our] spiritual consciousness. [We come] into consciousness of the river of life through the quickening of Spirit. [We] can be truly quickened with new life and vitalized in mind and body only by consciously contacting Spirit. This contact is made through prayer, meditation, and good works.

~ Charles Fillmore
Revealing Word, p. 122

Life

Overview

- Apostle: Judas
- Location: The Generative Organs, External Reproductive Organs
- Color: Red

LIFE is the ability to energize, vitalize, enliven, make whole.

From ego/personality: The ability to energize, vitalize, enliven, and make whole based on our senses, thoughts, feelings, and beliefs. We use LIFE to energize worthwhile projects and activities, and to manifest healing in our bodies. Conversely, LIFE can be used to energize troublesome projects like robbing a bank or manifest illness!

- *Underdeveloped Life* results in people who have little energy to accomplish anything. They are often apathetic, and may run into problems with illnesses and diseases.

- *Overdeveloped Life* results in people who demonstrate a frenetic kind of energy, coming across as hectic, feverish, and even be a bit chaotic. They have an unhealthy concern about their physical well-being, and may do things such as taking overdoses of vitamins, exercising to the extreme, and even experiencing burn-out.

From elevated consciousness: The ability to energize, vitalize, enliven, and make whole based on Ideas, Truths, Principles, and Laws that are Divine in nature. We use LIFE to energize and enliven our good intention and desire to be the best person and/or Christ we can be.

In the broadest and most important sense, Life is that great indefinable "something" that enlivens and energizes every living thing. We know that all living things, from viruses to human beings, clearly demonstrate life; however, scientists still cannot truly define what "life" actually is, other than perhaps a form of energy. Sure, we can describe in detail how a myriad of life forms replicate themselves, and yet we still cannot say with certainty what is happening. For humans, we say that the baby begins to "have life" with the union of the egg and sperm. And, yet, the egg and the sperm independently demonstrate this thing we call life.

If you have ever been in the presence of a person as they are making their transition, you probably know, at the moment of death, something invisible leaves the body. The physical body is still there, and it looks like the same person, but somehow you just know the person is no longer present. The "life" or energy is gone. But since energy cannot be destroyed, this "life" — this energy — must somehow continue; where and how we do not know.

There is also a similar, yet different way we speak of life. Have you ever used the phrase "breathe life into a project?" It means we give it an energy, a force, that generates excitement and results. We can also breathe life into the thoughts, feelings, ideas, and beliefs we hold. Clearly it is easy to see that all of the Powers/Abilities need to be brought into play in their most supportive and positive aspects, so we can enliven and energize our lives and our actions for the highest good for ourselves and others. In fact, you could say that the Ability of Life actually is used to energize all the other Abilities! That makes it difficult to discuss on its own ... but we're going to give it a shot!

Let's look at the Ability of Life first from the aspect of how we use it to energize projects, activities, and interests. It is easy to confuse Zeal and Life in this aspect, but if you will recall our chapter on Zeal we made a strong distinction between these two Abilities. We use the Ability Zeal to initiate and have passion about thoughts, ideas, beliefs, and projects. Zeal is the first stage of the rocket that gets it off the launching pad. Life is the second and even third stage of the rocket that gets it into orbit.

Most of us are enthusiastic about starting something new (which is our Zeal); once we get started, the Ability of Life enlivens and vitalizes that job or project.

Another very essential aspect of the Ability of Life is how it enlivens our mind and body, to achieve complete health, wholeness, and vitality. When you feel a cold coming on, you can claim and speak your Ability of Life to every cell and atom of your being, to manifest an energy that restores wholeness and health.

Life is underdeveloped in people who have little or no energy to engage in daily activities ... perhaps they are classic "couch potatoes!" They may even have the zeal and passion to get something going, but have little or no Life to energize and maintain it. Projects are done in a lack-luster way, and may not even be completed. These people may experience a higher level of illness in their lives, and run into problems with low stamina.

If you are like us, you can probably look back on your life and see the various energy levels you have experienced from the Ability of Life. There have been projects you were passionate about, and therefore energized at very high levels. Then there were projects you were more neutral about, and had difficulty doing anything more than just enough to get by. And finally, (let's all be honest here), there have been projects you were apathetic about or resistant to do, and as a result did not invest any energy in them at all. These are the projects you tend to procrastinate on, hoping someone else will do them, or they will simply disappear or die of neglect!

From a health and wholeness standpoint, an example of underdeveloped Life Power/Ability might be a man who constantly catches colds and flu bugs, because of low resistance. His thought pattern is probably something like this: "I always catch colds! I get every flu bug that comes along."

Life is overdeveloped in people who are restlessness, nervous, and hyperactive. They might energetically flit from one project to another, or be frenetic about completing something. Overdeveloped Life can be demonstrated in people that have "panic attacks," or those who simply cannot sit still. It could also be someone who is always excessively busy,

busy, busy ... but never really gets anything accomplished. When this becomes an extreme or chronic behavior, the person can reach the point of burning out. From a health and wholeness aspect, a person with an overdeveloped Ability of Life might obsess over doing all the things related to health, to the extreme. This person would work out at the gym three times a day, eat only raw vegetables, always have a bottle of water in their hand, and take mega doses of vitamins daily. They probably energize lots of worry thoughts, as well.

It is useful to review how the Ability of Life is used at various levels of consciousness:

1. **Unconscious Life:** based on a cause in subconscious mind which consists of beliefs that are not in our moment to moment awareness. A case in point would be a person who gives a lot of energy to self-deprecating remarks might have an unconscious need for outside validation.

2. **Conscious Life from our senses:** based on something in physicality we are gleaning through our sight, sound, scent, touch, and/or taste. A woman enjoys a massage because of the way it feels, the scent of the massage oil, and the soft background music; she invests energy in making massage a part of her regular routine.

3. **Conscious Life from our human personality:** based on thoughts, feelings, attitudes, and/or beliefs held in human consciousness. If you believe in the power of affirmations to contribute to your on-going health, you will create powerful affirmations and use them regularly to energize your body and deny giving power to illness.

4. **Conscious Life from our True Identity, or Higher Self:** based upon Divine Ideas, Laws, and Principles. At this level, we give energy to the pursuit of being the best person or Christ we can be. We invest time and energy studying the lives of people who have demonstrated a high level of consciousness, as well as learning about spiritual principles and laws. Most importantly, we enliven our thoughts and actions to apply what we have learned, to manifest results in our own lives.

Life:
Putting It Into Practice

Life — Activity One:

Part 1:

In your journal, respond to the following question by writing down as many answers as you can think of:

What am I giving energy to — and how is it serving me?

Part 2:

- Reflect on your answers, and assess what they are telling you about how you are showing up for life, and what you are experiencing.

- What would you like to change?

- In order to make that change, what do you need to give energy to, calling on your Ability of Life?

Life — Activity Two:

- As you think about the specific area you want to work on throughout this course, identify specific activities that have been difficult for you to work through and complete.
- How has the Ability of Life been involved, and how can you call on it to help you move toward success?
- How is the Ability of Life impacting your other 11 Abilities as you work on your specific area?

Example: Healthy Eating

The toughest area for me has been committing the time to fixing healthy meals at home. I get excited about it as I look through recipe books (lots of Zeal), and I even go to the store and buy the food. But then the food sits in the refrigerator and goes bad, because I can't seem to generate any interest in actually creating the meals.

I want to use my Ability of Faith to clearly claim the belief of the benefits of eating healthy; then I call on my Ability of Strength to stay the course through actually preparing the meals. And finally, I invoke my Ability of Life to enliven my ability to energetically prepare these healthy meals.

I will use affirmations to excite myself, and envision how these foods will help me create the healthy, attractive body I desire.

Life Affirmation:

I claim Life now. I use Life to energize and enliven my pursuit of being the best person and the best Christ I can be.

Case Example: Mary

*O*n the next few pages we explore one fictitious example to illustrate how the Powers/Abilities may be brought into play at the four levels of consciousness we explored in each of the preceding chapters. Each table focuses on a single level of conscious, and identifies each of the Twelve Abilities with the resulting action – how the Power/Ability "shows up" or is applied.

We will be using a fictitious person, Mary, who has been overweight for much of her life. Not only is Mary overweight, she grew up in a family where her parents and siblings are also overweight. They are definitely not height and weight proportionate. As witnessed by old family photographs, Mary's grandparents on both sides were also overweight.

We will begin by looking at Mary's subconscious or unconscious beliefs at the point where she finally decides – one more time – to lose weight. Yes, Mary has also been a yo-yo dieter/exerciser. We will look at how Mary uses each of the Powers/Abilities to maintain her current weight or even to gain more weight fueled by these subconscious beliefs. Yes, that's right! Since we cannot *not* use these Abilities, Mary, too, must have been using them to maintain her weight or gain more weight. These Powers/Abilities work … it is up to us to decide how we want to apply them. Moreover, these subconscious beliefs are the underlying reason her past attempts to diet and exercise have failed.

Subconscious Belief is the Cause

Mary is unaware of the causes of her being overweight because of one or more subconscious beliefs. Mary is totally unaware of two subconscious beliefs that fuel her being overweight:

- Belief that she inherited slow metabolish because of old family photographs showing all of her grandparents being overweight.
- Belief she is and will be heavy because she sees that everyone in her immediate family is overweight.

Power/Ability	Action (How the Power/Ability is used)
FAITH Believe	Mary's lifestyle choices are driven from these subconscious beliefs resulting in not eating right, eating too much of it, and does not exercise.
STRENGTH Persevere	Mary unconsciously uses Strength to support and hang onto her beliefs. This includes holding onto all the bad habits that maintain her weight or even gain more weight.
WISDOM Discern, apply	Mary unconsciously discerns and judges what to do in order to continue supporting these subconscious beliefs. It may seem strange and counter intuitive, but, She would "wisely" choose foods that keep her heavy as well as shun exercise - even avoiding the steps in favor of the elevator.
LOVE Desire, want, need, require	Mary unconsciously desires her subconscious beliefs. She uses Love to want and desire everything and anything that supports these beliefs. She desires the wrong foods and desires to be sedentary.
DOMINION Master	Mary unconsciously masters the art of eating poorly and not exercising. Also, she unconsciously dominates and controls any thoughts and feelings that are contrary to her subconscious beliefs.
IMAGINATION Visualize, conceptualize	Mary visualizes herself being overweight.
UNDERSTANDING Know	Mary unconsciously knows just what to do and what to avoid in order to support her subconscious beliefs.
WILL Choose	Mary unconsciously chooses foods based on what she knows (Understanding) and evaluates (Wisdom) to support her subconscious belief. Obviously, she chooses not to exercise.
ORDER Organize, adjust	Mary organizes her life insuring that there is no time to exercise nor time to eat right.
ZEAL Passion, start	It may seem odd, but, Mary is "passionate" about maintaining her beliefs and lifestyle. She is passionate about foods that are not good for her.
ELIMINATION Remove, deny	Through a litany of excuses, Mary eliminates, denies and dismisses any thoughts about eating right and getting exercise.
LIFE Enliven, vitalize	Mary is enlivening and vitalizing these beliefs with every choice she makes to eat poorly and not exercise. She enlivens her habits of eating poorly and not exercising.

Conscious Belief in an Outer Cause

Mary believes the only cause is from or in the outer, physical realm. She decides it is time, once again, to lose weight. Totally unaware of the subconscious beliefs the power she is giving them, Mary looks to her outer actions and the outer realm for the cause of her being overweight. With all the conscious information she has, Mary consciously thinks and feels the cause of her being overweight is because she does not eat right or get enough exercise. Mary now believes (Faith) she will lose weight if she only eats right and exercises.

Power/Ability	Action (How the Power/Ability is used)
FAITH Believe	Based on her belief that she is heavy simply because she does not eat right nor exercise, Mary begins a diet and exercise program, OR, she may choose surgical procedures: liposuction, lap-ban surgery, or laparoscopic obseity surgery to change her outer appearance.
STRENGTH Persevere	Mary uses Strength to stay the course with her decision to diet and exercise, OR, get surgery.
WISDOM Discern, apply	Mary uses Wisdom to discern how to exercise and diet, OR, to figure out the best doctors and surgery centers.
LOVE Desire, want, need, require	Mary uses Love to desire to lose weight. She also uses it to attract herself and desire to eat right and exercise, OR, to want and desire to get surgery.
DOMINION Master	Mary uses Dominion to master exercising and dieting, OR, to master what she needs to know and do in order to get surgery.
IMAGINATION Visualize, conceptualize	Mary use Imagination to see herself exercising and dieting as well as imagining what she will look like when she has lost the weight, OR, visualize herself doing what she needs to do to have the surgery.
UNDERSTANDING Know	Mary uses Understanding to know about various exercise programs, surgery, doctors and surgery centers.
WILL Choose	Mary uses Will to choose her belief in an outer cause as well as to choose a diet and exercise program, OR, to ultimately choose her doctor and surgery center
ORDER Organize, adjust	She uses Order to sequence and organize her life so that she can diet and exercise, OR, organizes her life and affairs so she can get surgery.
ZEAL Passion, start	She uses Zeal to start and be enthusiastic about her diet and exercise program, OR, to begin the process for surgery and be enthusiastic about it.
ELIMINATION Remove, deny	She uses Elimination to remove and deny any doubt she can do this as well as to eliminate inappropriate foods and habits, OR, to eliminate any fears and concerns about the surgery.
LIFE Enliven, vitalize	She uses Life to enliven and energize her diet and exercise programs, OR, to vitalize and energize the entire process of getting surgery.

Conscious Belief of a Cause in Consciousness

Mary notices, once again, that her diet and exercise plan begins to work and then she backslides and goes back to her old ways – it begins slowly and subtly and then accelerates until she is no longer dieting and exercises. This yo-yoing is inevitable since Mary is totally unaware of the subconscious beliefs that are "working against her." Or, more accurately, she is unconsciously using her Abilities to sabotage her efforts to lose weight. Her long standing subconscious beliefs are fueling her behaviors that work against her beliefs in dieting and exercise. For example, since the Ability of Strength is most effective when linked to something we firmly believe, her use of the Ability of Strength to stay the course with the new beliefs will not be as effective because the subconscious beliefs are still supporting the use of this Ability to stay the course with her former ways of eating and exercise.

Wisely, Mary begins to wonder and reflect on why all her efforts to diet and exercise do not work. She definitely knows that she is the one that decides to start eating poorly again, as well as to miss more and more days of exercise. Upon reflection and perhaps with some help from her therapist, Mary finally surfaces the subconscious beliefs. She becomes aware that she has been using her actions to hold and reinforce the beliefs that she inherited slow metabolism and that she will always be overweight because her entire family is overweight.

Mary now knows that she has work to do with the beliefs she is holding in consciousness in order to permanently lose weight. She also knows that she must disempower and eliminate the formerly subconscious beliefs while claiming a new belief.

Power/Ability	Action– How the Ability is used. Disempowering Old, Unwanted Beliefs	Action – How the Ability is used. Claiming New Beliefs
FAITH Believe	Now, Mary begins to disempower the unwanted beliefs: • Belief she inherited slow metabolism, because from the photograph she is able to see that all her grandparents were overweight. • Belief she is and will be heavy because she sees that everyone in her immediate family is overweight. (See the Power of Elimination).	Mary begins to claim the beliefs she wants: • I have a normal and health-promoting metabolism. • I am whole and healthy demonstrated by being height and weight proportionate Her deep realization of these beliefs is coupled with the use of affirmations such as, "I am whole and perfect, my weight is height and weight proportionate.
STRENGTH Persevere	Mary sticks with her inner work to transform her unwanted beliefs into wanted beliefs. She sticks with consistently using her denials. Every time she is aware of acting or even thinking in ways that support the unwanted beliefs she applies her denial.	Mary sticks with and perseveres with her inner work to claim the new beliefs by using her affirmations. She would also be sticking with her diet and exercise programs.

WISDOM Discern, apply	Mary has already discerned and judged which beliefs to remove. She knows how to use a denial.	Mary already wisely discerned which new beliefs she wants to claim, and wisely chooses her food and exercise. She knows how to use an affirmation.
LOVE Desire,want, need, require	Mary desires and wants to change her beliefs, thoughts and feelings.	She effortlessly desires and wants to support these new beliefs as well as to eat right and exercise.
DOMINION Master	Mary controls any thoughts and feelings that support her old beliefs.	Mary masters her new beliefs thoughts and feeling.
IMAGINATION Visualize, conceptualize	Mary conceptualizes how to release the beliefs she does not want, visualizing them flying out of her mind. She sees herself using her denials effectively.	Mary conceptualizes how to claim the new beliefs. She sees herself claiming the new beliefs.
UNDERSTANDING Know	Mary knows the beliefs she wants to let go. She knows how to construct a denial.	She knows the beliefs she wants to acquire and own. She knows how to construct an affirmation.
WILL Choose	Mary chooses/decides which beliefs to release. She decides to use denials.	She decides which new beliefs to clam. She decides to use affirmations.
ORDER Organize, adjust	Mary organizes her process to effectively disempower and eliminate old beliefs. She is aware of the Law of Divine Order: Mind-Idea-Expression.	Mary organizes her process to be effective at claiming and owning the new beliefs. She adjusts to changing situations in regards to her diet and exercise.
ZEAL Passion, start	Mary is passionate about disempowering and eliminating the old beliefs.	She is passionate and starts to claim the new beliefs as well as to start a new diet and exercise program.
ELIMINATION Remove, deny	Mary uses denials to disempower the unwanted beliefs. Example: I give no power to the belief I inherited low metabolism. I give no power to my family being heavy.	Mary uses her power of Elimination to remove and eliminate any thoughts of doubt about being able to complete her program as well as to maintain her weight loss. She also eliminates any foods or temptations to have foods that are not on her diet.
LIFE Enliven, vitalize	Mary enlivens and invigorates disempowering the beliefs she no longer wants.	Mary enlivens and invigorates claiming and owning the beliefs she wants.

Conscious Belief in a Higher Cause

While working to disempower her old subconscious beliefs, claim new beliefs and to continue her diet and exercise programs, Mary becomes aware that there is only One Power and One Presence, the Truth of What she is. Mary begins to believe in the Truth of her innate Christ Nature, even if this belief is merely the size of a mustard seed. She begins to loosen and disempower her Faith, her belief, in her personality or ego. As this new state of awareness gets more and more solidified, it affects the personality as well as the physical body.

Power/Ability	Action (How the Power/Ability is used)
FAITH Believe	Mary begins to own the belief in her innate Christ Nature.
STRENGTH Persevere	Mary stays the course and supports her belief in her Christ Nature no matter what her senses seem to be informing her.
WISDOM Discern, apply	Mary discerns when she is being Christ and when she is not. She applies what she knows about Christ Nature to her everyday life.
LOVE Desire, want, need, require	Mary desires and wants to be and demonstrate Christ. This includes desiring to be, do and say the things that demonstrate that she is Christ.
DOMINION Master	Mary masters the belief, thoughts and feelings in regard to Christ Consciousness. She also controls any thoughts and feelings to the contrary.
IMAGINATION Visualize, conceptualize	Mary visualizes and conceptualizes what it is like to be the best Christ she can be.
UNDERSTANDING Know	Mary knows both intellectually and spiritually what it is to be Christ.
WILL Choose	Mary chooses to be the best Christ she can be in the big picture as well in the moment to moment choices that support the belief and that decision.
ORDER Organize, adjust	Mary organizes and adjust her life so that she can be the best Christ she can be.
ZEAL Passion, start	Mary is passionate about this discovery as well as being passionate about being the best Christ she can be. She starts being the best Christ she can be.
ELIMINATION Remove, deny	Mary eliminates and denies any emerging thoughts, feelings and beliefs that work against her being the best Christ she can be.
LIFE Enliven, vitalize	Mary enlivens and vitalizes every aspect of her life so that she can be the best Christ she can be.

Appendix 1:
Historical Background on the Twelve Powers

Written by Eric Page, M.H.A.M.S.

Emma Curtis Hopkins, Annie Rix Militz, and other New Thought writers used the symbols of the numbers seven and twelve for [S]piritual [A]ttributes. Hopkins taught Militz as well as Charles and Myrtle Fillmore. Both Hopkins and Militz wrote for Unity. Hopkins operated a seminary in Chicago and lectured throughout the country. Militz worked at Unity before founding the California based Homes of Truth.

Information about Charles Fillmore's private experiences with the [T]welve [F]aculties is limited. Certainly the ideas of body centers were being discussed prior to Charles writing about the concepts. The Fillmores were part of a group of individuals who read and discussed concepts from eastern thought. Fillmore acknowledges Hinduism for the idea of seven centers or chakras in his writings.

Charles Fillmore does not mention colors related to the twelve powers in his 1930 book, *The Twelve Powers of Man*, though Unity writers were writing about colors. In her 1896 Unity article, "Twelve Lights," Mary E. Griswold explores [T]welve [S]piritual [A]ttributes represented by the colors of twelve jewels. A 1903 program given to graduates of an early Unity course includes affirmations and colors for seven objective centers. Colors were also included in a description of controlling centers in 1917. Colors are also outlined in a 1934 series in Unity magazine. One group of colors has been attributed to Joel Baehr in 1971. He noted that businesses were beginning to use colors for filing at the time. Baehr used a color key program at Unity Christ Church in St. Louis, Missouri and the color key program was adopted by the Association of Unity Churches International. [The Association carries 12 Power Candle sets for use in Unity Churches.]

Appendix 2:
Commentaries on Unregenerate, Degeneration, Generation, and Regeneration

Charles Fillmore, co-founder of Unity with his wife Myrtle, focused a great deal on the concept of regeneration. The Twelve Powers/Abilities is all about realizing our full Christ Potential. Regeneration focuses on one way we re-establish our awareness of our Christ Nature. These concepts will help clarify why regeneration is needed: the fall in consciousness, both collective and individual.

Unregenerate

The mortal mind is unregenerate when it is mired in error or sense consciousness and only gathers information through the senses. It then erroneously judges by appearance. It is a false state of mind. The unregenerate state precedes the awakening of the awareness of Truth. A person must move out of this unregenerate state in order to remember the Oneness.

Degeneration

Degeneration is the process of the "fall in consciousness." This began with the involvement in the pleasures of sensation and the seeking of guidance other than that of Source, or Christ Mind. This happened first in race or collective consciousness prior to any physicality.[1] The degeneration occurred gradually, resulting in the physical universe, physical bodies, and the entire experience of separation and error. Degeneration continues and is reinforced with every error thought and judgment.

Generation

Generation is a necessary aspect of living in this physical world in physical bodies. Generation is a genteel term used to define what we call procreation or sexual reproduction today. In *Dynamics for Living* (pg. 240) we find, "When man loses his body by death, the law of expression works within him for re-embodiment. He takes advantage of the Adam method of generation to regain a body. Divine mercy permits this process in order that man may have further opportunity to demonstrate Christ life." Then in Charles Fillmore's book, *The Twelve Powers,* we read, "Generation sustains and perpetuates the human; regeneration unfolds and glorifies the divine."

In another source, we find Charles saying:

> Now, as thinking people, we should inquire into the matter, and find out why we fall short, and what the necessary steps are to redemption, to change, to regenerate. Now, we know that generation is in large degree responsible for this present condition, because in generation everything has its origin. ...Then here we find ourselves in what might be called a degenerate state. Now, is this true of the Real [person], the [person] born in the image and likeness of God? You say at once, "why no!" (Lecture – First Steps in Regeneration, Charles Fillmore, Sunday, January 7, 1912).

Regeneration

Regeneration is the process by which we re-establish the awareness of our True Identity, or Christ Consciousness, through the quickening (enlivening) our innate Powers, or Abilities. Here are some excerpts from Unity magazine, that clarify the concept of Regeneration:

> Regeneration is neither a theory nor a fad; it is a spiritual ideal. It is not an opinion to be held, but a life to be lived. It is a spiritual quickening which purifies, refines, and exalts the soul [conscious and subconscious mind], and it gradually brings the mind and body under the dominion of the Christ Mind. It is a process of unfoldment. The culmination of this growth

is the Jesus Christ consciousness expressed as a resurrected life. Because regeneration is both a principle and the practice of the principle, it should not be confused with anybody's idea of what it might be, nor with anybody's opinion of what it should be. The real knowledge of it comes through the Holy Spirit[2] of Truth in your own heart. Follow it always, and you be led into Truth and nothing but the Truth (*Unity*, Jan. 1921: 54, #1, Kansas City, MO).

When the regeneration comes that Jesus referred to as "being born again," the New Birth will imply the being born out of worldly consciousness into a heavenly consciousness, out of the consciousness of the flesh into the consciousness of the Spirit, out of the consciousness of humanity into the consciousness of Divinity. This is what Paul means when he says; "If any man be in Christ, he is a new creature," or a new creation he might have put the passage in a different way. If Christ be in any man he is attuned to the consciousness of a new life, wherein the old things pass away before the coming newness of the Spirit of Life. Under the old order we were subject to the things of man's external world. Under the new order we rule all things, because we are only subject to the mind and will of the indwelling Spirit (C.B. Patterson, in "The Sunlight of Health," quoted from *Unity*, Apr. 1915: 42, #3, Kansas City, MO).

In Fillmore's system, regeneration seems to be always tied to the regeneration of the physical body.[3] Fillmore often referred to following Jesus in the regeneration and keeping his words so that we would never see death, physical death. He believed that Jesus demonstrated this:

As taught by Jesus, and by all spiritual teachers, the goal of man is the attainment of eternal life; the overcoming of physical death. The human race on this

planet will continue to die and be reborn until it learns
the law of right living, which will ultimate in a body so
healthy that it will never die. Jesus demonstrated this,
and He promised those who should follow Him in the
regeneration that they would never see death if they
should keep His words. Many Christians are getting
this understanding – that they have not attained eternal
life so long as they allow the body to continue in the
corruption that ends in death, and they are earnestly
beginning the appropriation, or eating and drinking, of
the life and substance of the Lord's body, until He
appears again in their regeneration organism (*Twelve
Powers*, Charles Fillmore, pg. 174).

It is a rather curious assertion that Jesus demonstrated having a physical body that never died. The gospels report that he died, rose from the
dead, and ascended. Some would contend that he did demonstrate that
the body did not need to stay dead. Even so, Jesus is not still around in
a physical body, nor has it been reported that any spiritual teachers have
demonstrated eternal life in the physical body. An eternal physical body
may be possible; however, it probably misses the point. It would seem
if we are to follow Jesus in the regeneration, it would mean we would end
up without a physical body. If the reports are true, Jesus definitely
demonstrated that!

Focusing on the physical body is focusing on effect rather than
Cause. Therefore it is best to go to Cause, focusing on the regeneration
of the Abilities in consciousness. The goal is the restoration of the awareness of Christ Consciousness and its full operation and application. Since
the body is the effect of causes in consciousness, then the body may and
can reflect this regenerative process.

The Powers are innate and therefore we must always be using them,
even if it is subconsciously or unconsciously. In the following quote,
Fillmore has some admonitions about how the Powers should *not* be
used, what needs to be overcome, how to develop the Powers, and ways
to use them effectively. He even seems to infer a person could choose not

to use them at all. And ironically, the ability to make that choice is the use of the Power of Will!

> We do not encourage those who still have worldly ambitions to take up the development of the twelve powers of man. You will be disappointed if you seek to use these superpowers to gain money (turn stones into bread), control others ("the kingdoms of the world... All things will I give thee"), or make a display of your power ("If thou art the Son of God, cast thyself down"). These are the temptations of the selfish ego, as recorded in the 4th chapter of Matthew, which Jesus had to overcome, and which all who follow Him "in the regeneration" have to overcome (*Twelve Powers*, Charles Fillmore, pg. 6).

> Unspeakable joy, glory, and eternal life are promised to those who with unselfish devotion strive to develop the Son of God consciousness. All the glories of the natural man are as nothing compared with the development of the spiritual man. The things of this world pass away, but the things of Spirit endure forever. In his flesh body, man may be compared to the caterpillar that is a mere worm of the earth, but it has, enfolded within it, a beautiful creature awaiting release from its material envelope (*Twelve Powers*, Charles Fillmore, pg. 6).

> Some metaphysical schools warn their students against the development of power, because they fear that it will be used in selfish, ambitious ways. It doubtless is true that the personal ego sometimes lays hold of the power faculty and uses it for selfish aggrandizement; we can readily see how what is called the Devil had origin. To be successful in the use of the power of Being, one must be obedient in exercising all the ideas that make man. If there is a an assumption of personal

power, Lucifer falls like "lightning from heaven," and the adverse or carnal mind goes to and fro in the earth. The casting out of these demons of personality formed a large part of the work of Jesus, and those who follow Him in the regeneration are confronted with similar states of mind and find it necessary to cast out the great demon selfishness, which claims to have power but is a liar and the father of lies (*Twelve Powers*, Charles Fillmore, pg. 66).

No disciple can do any great overcoming work without a certain realization of spiritual power, dominion, mastery. Without power, one easily gives up to temporal laws, man-made. The psychic atmosphere is filled with thoughts that are not in harmony with Divine Mind. These psychic thoughts are legion, and to overcome them one must be on one's guard. Jesus said, "Watch." This means that we should quicken our discernment and our ability to choose between the good and the evil. "And why even of yourselves judge you not what is right?" This wisdom of Spirit is man's through the all-knowing and all-discerning power of Spirit within him, and he need never fear going wrong if he listens to his divine intuition. "Ye shall know the truth, and the truth shall make you free." But man can never be free until he declares his freedom. Jesus said "I am from above." It is the prerogative of every man to make this declaration and thereby rise above the psychosis of mortal thought. Then do not fear to develop your power and mastery. They are not to be exercised on other people, but on yourself. "He that ruleth his spirit, [is more powerful] than he that taketh a city." Alexander cried because there were no more worlds to conquer, yet he had not conquered his own appetite, and died a drunkard at the age of thirty-three.

Today men are striving to acquire power through money, legislation, and man-made government, and falling short because they have not mastered themselves (*Twelve Powers*, Charles Fillmore, pg. 66).

What then, is necessary that we regenerate?

...In considering that matter [regeneration], we should first admit that there is [the] necessity of regeneration. If [humankind] is demonstrating the problem of life perfectly in [its] present consciousness, which is mind and body, why, [humankind] doesn't' need regeneration; but if [it] is falling short in that respect, humankind certainly needs awakening and reformation. This is the first step, and the final putting on of the body which they call the Christ ... (Lecture – First Steps in Regeneration, Charles Fillmore, Sunday, January 7, 1912).

...So the first thing necessary is, as I said, to know that we need regenerating, and the next is that we perceive the possibility, that we believe in the spiritual [person] and that we can bring [him or her] forth (Lecture – First Steps in Regeneration, Charles Fillmore, Sunday, January 7, 1912).

The method by which Jesus evolved from sense consciousness to God consciousness was, first, the recognition of the spiritual selfhood and a constant affirmation of its supremacy and power. Jesus loved to make the highest statements: "I and the Father are one." "All authority hath been given unto me in heaven and on earth." He made these statements, so we know that at the time He was fully aware of their reality. Secondly, by the power of His word He penetrated deeper into omnipresence and tapped the deepest resources of His mind, whereby He released the light, life, and substance of Spirit, which enabled Him to get the realiza-

tion that wholly united His consciousness with the
Father Mind (*Atom Smashing Power of Mind*, Charles
Fillmore, pg. 43).

...In making His great overcoming Jesus applied the
principles of Being scientifically, and He instructed
His followers to do as He did. ... Jesus differed from
other men in that He proved by His works that He was
the Son of God, while the average man is still striving
to attain that excellency (*Atom Smashing Power of
Mind*, Charles Fillmore, pg. 43).

...The reports by His followers of what He taught
clearly point to two subjects that He loved to discourse
upon. The first was the Son of God: He was the Son of
God. Secondly: We might all become as He was and
demonstrate our dominion by following Him in the
regeneration (*Atom Smashing Power of Mind*, Charles
Fillmore, pg. 43).

... He who has caught the significance of man, and
who and what man is, never allows himself to accept
any erroneous conclusions as to his final destiny. He
does however know there is a way provided by which
he can not only free himself from the claims of mate-
riality but also by his efforts open the way for many
others to do likewise. No person ever demonstrated his
God-given powers in even a small way but what he
helped others to do the same (*Atom Smashing Power
of Mind*, Charles Fillmore, pg. 43).

...The first step in every movement of the mind, and the
body also, is belief or faith in that thing. If we didn't
believe in the possibility of walking, we couldn't walk.
Everything has its conception in the mind. We believe
that [we are Spirit], that [Spirit is our Higher Self], the
[Real Self]; but we must put that into active operation

in the mind before we will demonstrate it. So, let us take for our prayer, our meditation in the Silence: I believe in the coming forth in me of the Mind and Body of Spirit (Lecture – First Steps in Regeneration, Charles Fillmore, Sunday, January 7, 1912).

We might all become as He [Jesus] was and demonstrate our dominion by following Him in the regeneration. In order to follow Jesus in the regeneration we must become better acquainted with the various phases of mind and how they function in and through the body (*Atom Smashing Power of Mind*, Charles Fillmore, pg 42).

In the regeneration, two states of mind are constantly at work. First comes the cleansing or denial state, in which all the error thoughts are eliminated. This includes forgiveness for sin committed and a general clearing up of the whole consciousness. The idea is to get back into the pure, natural [C]onsciousness of Spirit. ... In the first baptism, through the power of the word, the sense [person] is erased from consciousness, and the mind is purged and made ready for the second baptism.

In the second baptism, the creative [L]aw of [D]ivine [A]ffirmation, set into action by Mind, lights its fires at the center of [one's] being, and when thus kindled raises soul and body to a high degree of purity. This process is known as regeneration.

From this we discern that mental cleansing and the reforms that put the conscious mind in order are designed to prepare the way for that larger and more permanent consciousness which is to follow (*Dynamics for Living*, Charles Fillmore, pgs. 209 – 210).

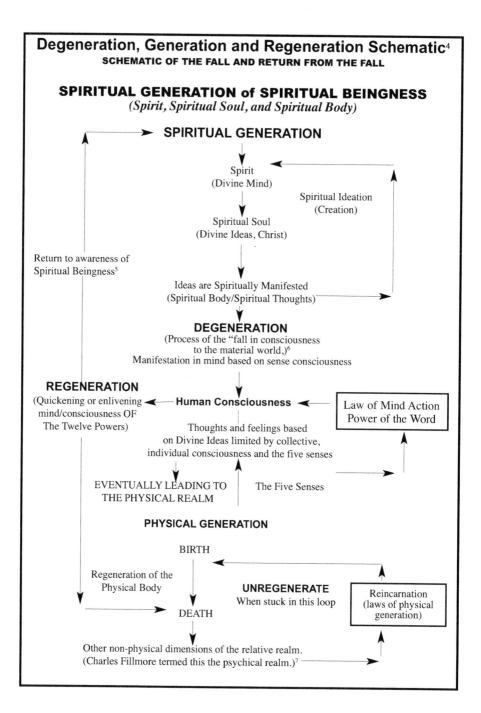

Degeneration, Generation and Regeneration Schematic[4]
SCHEMATIC OF THE FALL AND RETURN FROM THE FALL

SPIRITUAL GENERATION of SPIRITUAL BEINGNESS
(Spirit, Spiritual Soul, and Spiritual Body)

SPIRITUAL GENERATION

Spirit
(Divine Mind)

Spiritual Ideation
(Creation)

Spiritual Soul
(Divine Ideas, Christ)

Return to awareness of
Spiritual Beingness[5]

Ideas are Spiritually Manifested
(Spiritual Body/Spiritual Thoughts)

DEGENERATION
(Process of the "fall in consciousness
to the material world,)[6]
Manifestation in mind based on sense consciousness

REGENERATION
(Quickening or enlivening ◄— **Human Consciousness** ◄—
mind/consciousness OF
The Twelve Powers)

Law of Mind Action
Power of the Word

Thoughts and feelings based
on Divine Ideas limited by collective,
individual consciousness and the five senses

EVENTUALLY LEADING TO
THE PHYSICAL REALM

The Five Senses

PHYSICAL GENERATION

BIRTH

Regeneration of the
Physical Body

UNREGENERATE
When stuck in this loop

Reincarnation
(laws of physical
generation)

DEATH

Other non-physical dimensions of the relative realm.
(Charles Fillmore termed this the psychical realm.)[7]

Notes, Appendix 2:

1. "We are by birth a spiritual race, and we should never have known matter or material conditions if we had followed the leadings of our higher consciousness."(*Talks on Truth*, Charles Fillmore, pgs.163-164).

> The Garden of Eden or Paradise of God is in the ether, and we see that the 'fall of man' antedated the formation of this planet as we behold it geologically. Jesus recognized this when He said: 'And now, Father, glorify thou me with thine own self with the glory which I had with thee before the world was' (*Talks on Truth*, Charles Fillmore, pg. 163).

2. The Holy Spirit is often misunderstood, as it comes jam packed with the embedded theologies of our childhood. Unity writings by and large are not clear either. The Holy Spirit is not a person, entity, or being, any more than Divine Mind, or God, is. The Unity writings refer to It as He and sometime She, since Fillmore believe the Holy Spirit is the feminine aspect of God. It is defined in *The Revealing Word* as "The activity of God in a universal sense. The moving force in the universe taken as a whole. ... Holy Spirit and the Word--The Word is man's I AM identity [Christ, the Idea that is made up of ideas]. ...The Holy Spirit is the outpouring or activity of the living Word [Christ]." So, in a sense, the Holy Spirit is our experience of the activity of Divine Ideas (Christ) in Divine Mind (God). It is helpful to substitute the words "activity of God" or "the activity of the living Word (Christ)" wherever Holy Spirit is written to help avoid the pitfalls of embedded theology. The sentence that is footnoted then would read, "The real knowledge of it comes through the activity of God of Truth in your own heart" or "the real knowledge of it comes through the activity of the living Word of Truth in your own heart."

3. "Generation and death must give place to regeneration and eternal life. The necessity of rebirth must therefore pass away with all other make-shifts of the mortal [human]. It will have no place when [people] take advantage of the redeeming, regenerating life of Jesus Christ and quit dying" (Lecture – First Steps in Regeneration, Charles Fillmore, Sunday, January 7, 1912).

4. From Rev. Oren Evans Truth Kernal #2, Regeneration

5. In 21st Century language this might be better written Spiritual Beingness

6. Sense consciousness begins to limit / color / distort Divine Ideas

7. Where undeveloped souls rest while awaiting reincarnation

Appendix 3:
Additional Commentaries

Commentary on the Colors Associated with the Powers

The colors that are associated with the Twelve Powers were created by Rev. Joel Behr many years ago. They were not part of the original system as put forth by Charles Fillmore. Many find it useful to have a color associated with a Power, or Ability; others do not. A person does not have to relate to the color system in order to understand and apply the Powers, or Abilities.

Commentary on the Disciples and the Powers

The relation of the twelve disciples to the Twelve Powers arises from Charles Fillmore's the metaphysical interpretation of the Bible. It is definitely an integral part of Charles Fillmore's system. Fillmore presents the Twelve Powers in the order in which Jesus called his disciples. He also noted when there was already an association between the disciples. For example, Jesus called Peter and Andrew together. Thus, Faith and Strength work together. The association of a particular disciple and a Power sometimes is pretty obvious. For example, Peter demonstrated Faith when Jesus asked him to walk on the water. Other ones seem like a stretch. The usefulness of this part of the system is up to you. However, in Unity, there are a few disciples and the associated Power that are mentioned on a regular basis and are therefore good to know such as Peter (Faith), John (Love), Phillip (Power) and Andrew (Strength).

Commentary on the Body Locations Associated with the Powers

Many people find these associations to be quite a stretch. However, a particular logic is found when taken in the context of the Unity teachings.

1. Everything begins in Divine Mind as Divine Ideas.
2. The physical body is manifested using Divine Ideas according to the level of consciousness manifesting it.[1]
3. Therefore there must be a center associated with each Power in the body.

Charles Fillmore believed that each of these centers enlivens and controls the associated functions in and around that location. For example, the Power of Power (Dominion or Mastery) is located in the throat, base of the tongue and larynx. The Power of Power had a part to play in manifesting this area of the body and continues to have an influence at that location. Thus, as one spiritualizes the Power and its associated location, regeneration occurs Spiritually, mentally and physically. Like the disciples, some of the associations make sense like Elimination being in the lower bowel; others may not. Interestingly, in some cases recent science is backing up Fillmore in regards to the locations he discerned. Fillmore located the Power of Will along with Understanding in the front fore brain. Recently, scientific studies on the brain have located the will in this part of the brain!

Having a color and a body location can be a useful way to focus on a Power during Meditation; or even while consciously utilizing one during everyday waking life. This can be an important part of the process of regeneration at all levels (Spiritual, mental and physical).

Notes, Appendix 4:
1. Body - The outer expression of consciousness; the precipitation of the thinking part of man. God created the idea of the body of man as a self-perpetuating, self-renewing organism, which man reconstructs into his personal body. God creates the body idea, or divine idea, and man, by his thinking, makes it manifest. As God created man in His image and likeness by the power of His word, so man, as God's image and likeness, projects his body by the same power. (*The Revealing Word*, pg. 26)

Appendix 4: Twelve Powers/Abilities Summary Chart

POWER	ABILITY TO	From sense consciousness / Personal Consciousness	From Higher Consciousness / Spiritual Awareness
Faith	Believe, intuit, perceive, to have conviction, to "hear"	The ability to believe erroneously based on sense consciousness, error thoughts and feelings. Believing in things of the outer realm. "Belief, human intuition, conviction, opinion."	The ability to believe and perceive the Reality of Divine Ideas, Truths, Principles and Laws. "Conviction, Spiritual Intuition"
I claim my Power of Faith now. I perceive, and spiritual intuit Divine Ideas.			
Strength	Endure, stay the course, last, be persistent, persevere, to be stable	The ability to endure and hold onto based on senses consciousness, error thoughts and feelings. Hanging onto things in the outer realm. "stubbornness, forcefulness, obsessive compulsive."	The ability to persevere and hold onto Divine Ideas, Truths, Principles and Laws. "Endurance, Perseverance"
I claim my Power of Strength now. I hold onto and stay the course based on Divine Ideas despite outer appearances.			
Judgment / Wisdom / Discernment	Judge, evaluate, discern, be wise, appraise, to know how to, to apply what you know	The ability to judge and evaluate based on sense consciousness, error thoughts and feelings. Judging based on worldly standards. "Judging, judgmental, discrimination, shrewdness."	The ability to discern and be wise based on Divine Ideas, Truths, Principles and Laws. The ability to know how to use what we Spiritually Understand. "Discerning, Being Wise"
I claim my Power of Wisdom now. I wisely know how to use Divine Ideas.			
Love	Harmonize, unify, desire, attract oneself to, feel affection for	The ability to attract ourselves to the ideas, thoughts, and things based on sense consciousness, erroneous thoughts and feelings. Attracting ourselves to things and people in the outer realm. "Craving, needing, neediness. The ability to harmonize and unify everything to match what we attract ourselves to based on sense consciousness. The ability to desire or feel affection for another person, object or situation based on the senses "Lust, fatal attraction, obsession."	The ability to attract ourselves to Divine Ideas, Truths, Principles and Laws. The ability to harmonize and unify everything to match Divine Ideas, Principles and Laws. (Link with Wisdom and Understanding)
I claim my Power of Love now. I harmonize and unify my life from Divine Ideas.			
Power/Dominion	Master, dominate, control	The ability to master and dominate thoughts and feelings based on sense consciousness, erroneous thoughts and feelings. Dominating based on the outer realm. "Domineering, controlling"	The ability to have dominion and mastery over thoughts and feelings based on Divine Ideas, Truths, Principles and Laws.
I claim my Power of Dominion now. I have dominion over all my beliefs, ideas, thoughts and action based on Divine Ideas.			
Imagination	Image, picture, conceptualize, envision, dream	The ability to envision all sorts of errors and horrors based on sense consciousness, erroneous thoughts and feelings. Envisioning based on the outer realm. "Waking nightmares, fantasy, delusion."	The ability to envision and conceptualize Divine Ideas, Truths, Principles and Laws. (Linked with Faith)
I claim my Power of Imagination now. I give form and shape to Divine Ideas and Substance.			

Understanding	Know, perceive, comprehend and apprehend.	The ability to know and comprehend based on sense consciousness, error thoughts and feelings. The ability to know based on the outer, relative realm. "Human knowledge, human knowing."	The ability to know, comprehend and apprehend the laws of thought and the relation of ideas (Divine Ideas, Truths, Principle and Laws) one to the other. "Spiritual Knowledge"
I claim my Power of Understanding now. I know Divine Ideas.			
Will	Choose, decide, command, lead, determine	The ability to choose and lead based on sense consciousness, the "outer realm." "willfulness, wrong-headedness, obstinacy."	The ability to choose and lead based on Divine Ideas, Truths, Principles and Laws. "Will"
I claim my Power of Will now. I choose, decide and lead based on Divine Ideas.			
Order	Organize, balance, sequence, adjust	The ability to organize, sequence, balance and/or adjust based on sense consciousness, erroneous ideas, thoughts, beliefs and feelings. Organization based on the outer realm. "Obsessive about orderliness, obsessive about details, anal retentive." As Divine Order (mind-idea-expression) it is forming based on sense and personal consciousness.	The ability to organize, balance, sequence and/or adjust according to and based on Divine Ideas, Truths, Principles and Laws. As Divine Order (mind-idea-expression) it is creating based from Spiritual Awareness/Higher Consciousness more purely using Divine Ideas.
I claim my Power of Order now. I organize and balance my life according to Divine Ideas.			
Zeal	Be enthusiastic, be passionate, start, motivate... The urge and impulse behind all things.	The ability to be enthusiastic and passionate based on sense consciousness, error thoughts and feelings. "Zealous, impulsive, overly ambitious, ruthless, compulsive"	The ability to be passionate and enthusiastic about Divine Ideas, Truths, Principles and Laws. "Passionate"
I claim my Power of Zeal now. I am passionate and enthusiastic about Divine Ideas.			
Elimination / Renunciation	Release, remove, denounce, deny; let go	The ability to release, deny and let go based on sense consciousness, error thoughts and feelings. Releasing based on the outer realm. "Purging, eradication, wasteful."	The ability to release, deny and let go false ideas, error thoughts and "lesser good" based on Spiritual Awareness/Higher Consciousness
I claim my Power of Elimination now. I deny and eliminate any limiting beliefs, ideas, thoughts, feelings and attitudes.			
Life	Energize, vitalize, enliven, animate and envigorate	The ability to vitalize and energize erroneous ideas and thoughts based on sense consciousness, error thoughts and feelings. Energizing based on the outer realm. "Frenetic, hectic, feverish, chaotic."	The ability to enliven and energize Divine Ideas, Truths, Principles and Laws.
I claim my Power of Life now. I vitalize and energy all that I think and do based on Divine Ideas.			

Appendix 5: Twelve Powers with Adverse Meanings

The Twelve Powers / Faculties/ Abilities

Power	Ability to	Location	Disciple	Color
Faith	believe, intuit [belief based on the senses]	Pineal Gland	Peter	Blue
Strength	endure, stay the course, to last, to be persistent, persevere, to be stable [stubbornness, forcefulness, obsessive compulsive]	Small of the back	Andrew	Spring Green
Judgment	evaluate, discern, be wise, appraise [judgmental, discrimination, shrewdness]	Pit of the stomach	James Z.	Yellow
Love	harmonize, unify, attract to [craving, neediness, lust, fatal attraction]	Back of the heart	John	Pink
Power	master, dominate, control [domineering, controlling]	Base of tongue, voice box	Philip	Purple
Imagination	image, conceptualize, envision [waking "nightmares", fantasy, delusion]	Between the eyes	Bartholomew	Light Blue
Understanding	know, perceive [human knowing, perception based on the senses]	Front brain	Thomas	Gold
Will	Choose, decide [willfulness, wrong-headedness, obstinacy, don't confuse me with the facts]	Front brain	Matthew	Silver
Order	organize, sequence, adjust [obsessive compulsive, anal retentive, obsessive about details, "dis-orderly", slovenly]	Navel	James A.	Olive Green
Zeal	start, motivate, be passionate, be enthusiastic [zealous, impulsive, ruthless, compulsive, overly ambitious]	Medulla, brain stem	Simon C.	Orange
Elimination	release, remove, denounce [wasteful, purging, eradication, throwing the baby out with the bath water]	Lower abdominal region	Thaddeus	Russet
Life	energize, vitalize, enliven [frenetic, hectic, feverish, chaotic, sloth-like, low-energy]	Generative center, external reproductive organs	Judas	Red

About the Authors ~

Rev. Dr. Paul Hasselbeck currently serves as the Dean, Spiritual Education and Enrichment, at Unity Village, MO. He helped found the only English-speaking Unity Church in Puerto Rico. Dr. Hasselbeck is the author of several books, including *Point of Power: Practical Metaphysics to Help You Transform Your Life and Realize Your Magnificence* (published in English and Spanish) and *Heart-centered Metaphysics: A Deeper Look at Unity Teachings*. Paul's internet radio program, Metaphysical Romp, airs live Tuesdays at 2 p.m. CT on www.unity.fm. The programs are also available as downloadable files. In his free time, Paul enjoys working out, surfing eBay, collecting vintage art pottery, and enjoying a flock of exotic birds. He lives in Kansas City with his partner, Martin.

Rev. Dr. Cher Holton is currently co-minister (with her husband Rev. Dr. Bil Holton) of the Unity Spiritual Life Center in Durham, NC. In addition to her work within Unity, Dr. Holton also conducts unique Turbo-Training™ and Retreat Forward™ programs for corporate clients around the world, heping them bring harmony to life. She is one of less than two dozen professionals world-wide  who have earned both the Certified Speaking Professional and the Certified Management Consultant designations. She has authored several books, including *Living at the Speed of Life: Staying in Control in a World Gone Bonkers!* In her spare time, Cher enjoys her three incredible grandchildren, mystery and suspense novels, the theatre, and ballroom dancing (she and Bil have won national awards as an amateur student couple).

Other Books/Products by These Authors:

Co-authored by Dr. Hasselbeck and Dr. Holton:
PowerUp™: A Twelve Powers Inspirational Card Set

Other Books by Dr. Paul Hasselbeck:

Point of Power: Practical Metaphysics to Help You Transform Your Life and Realize Your Magnificence
Heart-Centered Metaphysics: A Deeper Look at Unity Teachings
Get Over It: The Truth About What You Know That Just Ain't So!*
Get Over These, Too! More Truth About What You Know That Just Ain't So!*
*Co-authored with Dr. Bil Holton

Other Books by Dr. Cher Holton

Living at the Speed of Life: Staying in Control in a World Gone Bonkers!
The Manager's Short Course to a Long Career*
From Ballroom to Bottom Line—in business and in life*
Business Prayers for Millennium Managers*
Suppose ... Questions to Turbo-Charge Your Business and Your Life*
Crackerjack Choices: 200 of the Best Choices You Will Ever Make*
Right thoughts, Right Choices, Right Actions: 200 of the Best Choices Unity People Will Ever Make*
*Co-authored with Dr. Bil Holton

To order additional copies of this book, and other books by these authors, or to request information about scheduling either of them for speaking engagements, we invite you to contact them at:

Rev. Dr. Paul Hasselbeck: hasselbeckap@unityonline.org
Rev. Dr. Cher Holton: cher@holtonconsulting.com

CPSIA information can be obtained
at www.ICGtesting.com
Printed in the USA
FSOW03n1419041017
39259FS